LOCATING
HOME

**The First
African-Canadian**
Novel and
Verse Collections

LOCATING
HOME

Selected and Introduced
by
George Elliott
Clarke

Tightrope Books
#207-2 College Street,
Toronto Ontario, Canada M5G 1K3
tightropebooks.com
bookinfo@tightropebooks.com

COPY EDITOR: Deanna Janovski
COVER PHOTO: Title: Augustus Adams in his front yard in Sandwich, 1906 from the Ministry of Government Services, Archives of Ontario
COVER & BOOK DESIGN: David Jang

FONTS USED IN THE BOOK:
The Introduction was set in 10 pt ITC Berkeley Old Style
Clarence and Corinne was set in 10.5 pt Cochin
The Album of a Heart was set in 10 pt Janson
Citadel was set in 10 pt ITC Esprit

   Canada Council   Conseil des arts
for the Arts   du Canada

Produced with the assistance of the Canada Council for the Arts and the Ontario Arts Council.

Library and Archives Canada Cataloguing in Publication

Locating home / George Elliott Clarke, editor.

ISBN 978-1-988040-21-9 (softcover)

1. Canadian literature (English)--Black Canadian, authors.
2. Canadian literature (English). I. Clarke, George Elliott, 1960-, editor

PS8235.B53L63 2017   C810.8'0896071   C2017-905305-1

❄

Viens-tu du ciel profond ou sors-tu de l'abîme,
          Ô Beauté?
—Charles Baudelaire, "Hymne à la Beauté"

ACKNOWLEDGEMENTS

I wish to thank Jim Nason of Tightrope Books for so enthusiastically accepting this publishing project when I proposed it to him back in the summer of 2015. I also need to thank the Tightrope Press insurgents and activists, artistes and intellectuals, namely, David Jang, Deanna Janovski, and Heather Wood. They've made this book look *damn* good and, in doing so, have honoured powerfully the pioneer African-Canadian authors gathered here.

I also need to send a shout out back two decades, to a conference on "The History of the Book in Canada/Histoire de l'imprimé au Canada," held at the National Library of Canada/Bibliothèque nationale du Canada, in Ottawa, Ontario, on May 24, 1997. It was on that date and in that place that my Introduction herein was first presented as a conference paper, entitled, "Getting the Word Out: Self-Publication and the Development of African-Canadian Literature."

My most vital interlocutor regarding the poetry of Anna Minerva Henderson, these past twenty years, has been the independent scholar, Ms. Adrienne Shadd. I bow again to her superb scholarship in recovering Henderson's poetry and theorizing about her poetics.

I also recognize herein the E.J. Pratt Professorship of the University of Toronto, backed by Victoria University, and Dr. Sonia Labatt, who grant me *mucho*-appreciated, requisite research and travel funds. Finally, I thank exuberantly Ms. Giovanna Riccio for her spirited, loving encouragement of my every jot and tittle—and for her critical correction of my moral errors.

George Elliott Clarke
Toronto (ON) 31 *octobre mmxvii*

TABLE OF CONTENTS

Toward Establishing an —or *the*—"Archive" of African-Canadian Literature

George Elliott Clarke[i]

No history is straightforward (unless it is over), but some are more disorderly than others.[ii] Consider, for instance, the chronicle of a literature that I describe as "African-Canadian" but that some others prefer to label—as is their wont—as "Black Canadian." For contemporary critics reviewing or studying works of Canadian-African/"Negro" provenance, the blatant—and salutary—bias is to understand them as a "recent" categorization, as a "now" literature penned by "arrived" writers (like the Canadian-by-choice Dionne Brand [1953-] or the Canadian-by-birth Lawrence Hill [1957-]). For many readers—and even for some scholars— there is no African/Black Canadian literature, if we mean "creative writing," before "Bajan" native Austin Chesterfield Clarke's first novel appears in 1964. There's a wanton simplicity in such a chronological and cultural-critical assertion: One is freed from having to spelunk into the darkest, dustiest, dirtiest depths of archives.[iii] Furthermore, one may presume—with one's readers—that even if there are earlier novels out there, authored by African-heritage colonial settlers of British North America or by citizens of the Dominion of Canada, they cannot

---

i   An earlier version of this introduction appears in *Editing as Cultural Practice in Canada*, edited by Dean Irvine and Smaro Kamboureli (2016). I acknowledge gratefully the permission of the original publisher, Wilfrid Laurier University Press, to allow my herein revised essay to introduce this anthology.

ii US philosopher of history Hayden White observes, "we require a history that will educate us to discontinuity more than ever before; for discontinuity, disruption, and chaos is our lot" (50). Disjuncture is certainly the fate of any narrative of African-Canadian literature.

iii Yet, we must realize, with Jacques Derrida, "There is no political power without control of the archive, if not of memory" (qtd in Schultz 103).

be worth recovering. After all, what could such dead-and-buried works have to say to us today that is of any import, even as sociology, never mind as story? The fine writer and scholar M. NourbeSe Philip expresses precisely such a *noble* reservation when she feelingly complains of "a great Canadian void" (*Frontiers* 45), that is to say, the absence of significant, Black Canadian literary production before the onset of significant Afro-Caribbean immigration, 1955-present. "Until now"—essentially from the 1970s onwards—she *seems* to say, there is no African-Canadian literary history that is lustrous enough to bear reading, reprinting, and even riffing upon. A peculiar amnesia underscores such pronouncements. As antidote, one must recall Michel Foucault's assertion that "a revolutionary undertaking is directed against the rule of 'until now'" (*Language* 233), meaning, presumably, that a revolutionary must appreciate that to deem existing circumstances as "new" is propaganda against insurgency.[iv] In other words, there are always precedents, antecedents, ancestors. However, it is seldom in the interest of the ruling class or its disciples to *remember*, let alone applaud, the cultural works of disempowered minorities. Thus, again, when Philip argues that early African-Canadian writing (sermons and religious tracts) is "not literature" (*Genealogy* 73n22), one feels her consternation that black settlers and illiterate ex-slaves in early Canada did not—or could not—bother to author novels, plays, and verse collections. Indeed, there are only a few extant slave narratives that one can list, unblushingly, as "Canadian" (either by authorship or by publication). Formidably then, Philip calls into question the rationale for exhuming early black writing in Canada and daring to call it "literature," when it is obviously "less than" such. This point is cogent if we set, say, Phillis Wheatley, the first African-American poet to publish a book (1773), against a figure like Susannah (Susana) Smith, once of Virginia, then of Nova Scotia, and finally of Sierra Leone, who wrote—or spoke and saw transcribed—a letter, dated May 12, 1792, asking for "Sope" (Fyfe 24). To compare Wheatley's achievement to Smith's is to compare letterpress printing with handwriting. Nevertheless, one might posit that "literature" is not strictly a synonym for "creative writing," and recognize that religious texts—even sermons—may find themselves

iv   The tyranny of the new is that it pretends that hard-fought victories are "miracles" and that routs are "preordained"; that history is not made, but "born."

anthologized and their (collective) authors taught in university English classes. Canons do, it would appear, interpenetrate, not necessarily "each after its own kind," but rather in flagrant miscegenation, so that the Holy Bible migrates from Departments of Theology to English classes where it appears as "The Bible as Literature," or, say, *The Autobiography of Malcolm X* (1965) violates the boundaries of political science and history and ends up in a graduate English seminar. In this Age of Deconstruction, who can be sure about what texts to exclude *qua* literature, anyway? (Any text can be literature, but only the *studied* text constitutes "good" literature?) To sum up my preamble here, the *project* of properly constituting an African/ Black Canadian literature is one that entails mining archives, both to extract "legitimate" texts and authors for study, but also to reconstitute history as a base—shifty, yes, but not an abyss.ᵛ Indeed, I think we need to understand that the project of assembling any anthology is, implicitly (and sometimes explicitly), a challenge to the canonical parameters established by previous anthologies, whether they be—to refer to my own project—African-Canadian, African-American, Caribbean, British, French, French-colonial, and so on. To propose a national anthology of "early" African-Canadian literature is to also push against (or even push aside) previous anthologies of *other* literatures or canons.

To oppose any suggestion that, by advocating retrieval of the antique and the forgotten and the lost, I am also fetishizing, ironically, the "new," the "discovery," I will remark that I follow Smaro Kamboureli's sage comment in her introduction to her anthology, *Making a Difference: Canadian Multicultural Literature* (1996), that her attempt to offer "a historical overview" is intended to dispel "the notion that multicultural writing is only a recent phenomenon" (xxii). At the same time, she is conscious that "Any anthology that intends to offer a historical overview can only function as an allegory of literary history, can only map out yet another narrative path by which we can enter that history" (xxii). Bearing these *bons mots* in mind, I want to argue that to catalogue black books and black writers, of Canadian location, from before the 1960s, is to also identify "firsts": the first poets, playwrights, and novelists. By doing so, we

---

v   As Marianne Korn has said in her study of US poet Ezra Pound, "historical truth is not necessarily fact to be received, simple and unchanged, unmediated…: but rather a 'rag-bag' of details whose status is uncertain, whose truths are unclear, and whose causal links have vanished" [8].

also note their initial grappling with the pernicious subtlety of Canadian racism, in both its social and state guises, and ascertain their strategies for presenting themselves and representing their communities despite official narratives that, resenting their presence, strove to erase their existence. Should we examine these debut "Black Canuck"[vi] scribes, we might also find that their works pioneer trends, leitmotifs, ethics, orthographies, and themes still *au courant* within *our* literature.

Notwithstanding the preceding paragraphs, one recognizes that the scholar or historian of African-Canadian literature is stuck with the problem of having to declare a genesis wherever he or she feels best able to position it (while holding—strictly—that all such origins are never fixed). Our strategy here affirms the Franco-Ontarian critic René Dionne's intuition in *La Littérature régionale aux confins de l'histoire at de la géographie* (1993) that *"une littérature régionale possède déja un corpus d'oeuvres au moment où ses promoteurs la proclament comme un domaine littéraire particulier"* (38). Just as the critic of Franco-Ontarian—or Acadien or Québécois—literature must prove the existence of such literatures by carving them out of the larger corpus of French, French-Canadian, and world francophone literature, so must the student of Black Canadian writing seize his or her texts from the libraries and canons of Africa, African America, the Caribbean, South America, Europe, and European Canada. Ultimately, one declares his or her authority to claim a text or writer as constitutive of a "new" régime of reading, and one must stand prepared to defend this syllabus, just as the founders of a "new" nation must first declare and then defend its existence. In a landmark article, African-American scholar Nahum Dimitri Chandler assures us, "In order to displace hegemonic institutions"—such as, let us say, totemic canons—"one can only carry out a full displacement by crossing the threshold from open criticism to a declaration of authority" (87). To fuse—but not confuse—the thought of Dionne and Chandler, African/Black Canadian literature truly *arrives* as the consequence of brazen, authoritarian, unilateral, retroactive, self-conscious, and defensive

---

vi   I am deliberately jocular here, for I want to normalize the notion of people of African provenance being also, simultaneously, Canadian. So, if there are Canucks, to use the jocular term, so can there be Black Canucks. Of course, African-Canadian is a more "correct" phrase, though Black Canadian is also fine. To refer to the historical black communities of the Maritime provinces, especially Nova Scotia, I do use, occasionally, my neologism, "Africadian[s]," who reside, thus, in "Africadia."

(offensive?) annunciation of a canon and a chronology. In other words, ya gotta come with the truth—or just sit your ass down: "Without assuming power according to some existing institution within the status quo, any project of criticism is always open to a quite worldly and unkind intervention" (87). If you don't search and research, you don't found no "church." Then again, to cite Richard Sher, "each book has its own peculiar way of coming into the world and inhabiting it" (58). It's the same thing for *a* literature.

In *Odysseys Home: Mapping African-Canadian Literature* (2002), I compiled a bibliography of the literature, canvassing anglophone and francophone texts, from 1785 to 2001-2002. Introducing the compilation, I recorded a few "firsts," despite the good-intentioned objections of scholar Rinaldo Walcott, who urges that Black Canadian intellectuals "refuse the seductions of 'firstness' and engage in critique, dialogue and debate, which are always much more sustaining than celebrations of originality" (xiv).[vii] Yet, the novels of Martin Robison Delany and Amelia Etta Hall Johnson, the poetry of Nathaniel Dett and Anna Minerva Henderson, and the drama of Lennox Brown, to use only a few, English-language examples, serve to "introduce"—"inaugurate"—a resonant, Canuck interrogation of "blackness" and "national" identity, and these concerns *still* animate African/Black Canadian writers and their critics "now." Moreover, these authors step into the "void" (cf. Philip) and assume both authority to speak and, indeed, to disrupt or dispute discourses, usually negative, about Africa and Africans and "Negro" *being*.[viii] Decades intervene between these authors, and they experience different socio-economic and political conditions. Somehow, however, they address consistently questions that bedevil us persistently. Excepting the dyed-in-the-wool African-American Delany, these writers sure are—yep—obscure. Nevertheless, they jet an inkling of Black Canuck literature, even if we are oblivious to this achievement. Undeniably, these "accu(r)sed" progenitors of African-Canadian literature penned a set of esoteric publications, all existing in splendid independence from each

vii   What is so scary about the endeavour to recover early African-Canadian texts and writers? What is it that we do not want them to say to us? That *we* are *not* the "first"?

viii Relevant here is Kathy Lou Schultz's interpretation of African-American poet Langston Hughes's political intent: "Hughes writes into the voids in official records, making his own histories, highlighting the fact that the construction of the archive—of memory—must constantly be tended" (103).

other, but all also participating in the conversations of their times, from abolitionism to temperance, from Afrocentrism to integration, and also echoing respective literary movements, from romanticism to modernism. Still, these writers are also projections to black readers of the future, though not necessarily (or only) African Canadians.

Crucially, one *echt* distinction between early African-American and African-Canadian authors is that the former can hope for a domestic (or naturalized) readership, while the latter, generally, cannot. For this reason, seldom do most early African-Canadian authors appeal[ix] to Canadians of any complexion, except obliquely. (The startling exception is Henderson, though she, pointedly, in speaking to her immediate New Brunswick audience, veils her racial identity and marginalizes "blackness.") Thus, when Franck Fouché publishes his poetry collection, *Message*, in Port-au-Prince, Haiti, in 1946, he has no reason to expect a bibliographer to come along, sixty-five years later, to claim his work, addressed first to Haitians, then to French readers, and finally to African Americans, as the first francophone African-Canadian work of verse. Yet, to read *Message* from an African-Canadian vantage point lends it more value than to read it simply as a mid-century Haitian—later Haitian-Canadian—poet's debut. Frankly, even if Fouché were regarded in Haiti as a middling writer of piddling notice, he would still merit the cultish fandom of African-Canadian scholars and readers for having been the first proto-Afro-Canadian to author—in French—a verse collection *and* a play.

Another oddity that marks early African-Canadian texts is that rarely are they *real* "books." Instead, one novel is a newspaper serial (Delany's *Blake*), pamphlet-length chapbooks serve as poetry collections (see Henderson's *Citadel*), and mimeographed typescripts represent drama (see Brown's plays). To turn to Sher again, he registers that "Each [book] is unique, and none can be made to fit a prefabricated mold" (58). Who's to say that we cannot treat "non-books" as if they were—eccentric—books? Sher assures us "books serve as homes for text, but they are also physical artifacts, commodities, status symbols, and more. They come in a variety of sizes and shapes, are published and marketed in different ways, and vary in other respects …" (42). It would be repressive to rule out early African/Black texts as "books" just because they lack cloth

ix   In both senses—aggressive and responsive …

covers. Too, the physical status—or artifact—of the "book" is an essential aspect of its meaning, purpose, and audience "pivoting." Even so, all African-Canadian literary production desiring public consumption shares in the idea that print creates, says Claire Hoertz Badaracco, "a public culture of aesthetic and political significance" (15). For the foundational literary writers of Black Canuck presence, that "public culture" is debates around slavery, family life, racism, colonialism, temperance, but also aesthetics and existentialism. In *Trading Words: Poetry, Typography, and Illustrated Books in the Modern Literary Economy* (1995), Badaracco observes that "Poets, typographers, book designers, advertising illustrators, printers, publicists, and journalists share a common purpose in the modern literary economy—persuasion linked with sales" (195). If we extend the notion of African-Canadian modernity back to 1859 when Delany's *Blake* is serialized and forward to 1965 when Brown's first play, *The Captive*, is issued by the Ottawa Little Theatre, we affirm that "persuasion"—even propaganda—is the principal interest of the "first" African-Canadian texts. Arguably, then, even Susannah Smith's humble request for "Sope" is not distinct from Amelia Johnson's plea for temperance and obedience to Anglo-Protestant Christian morality or Henderson's implicit integrationism.

To open up the book-format of Martin Robison Delany's *Blake; or, The Huts of America: A Tale of the Mississippi Valley, the Southern United States, and Cuba*, arguably the first African-Canadian novel, is to audit an expression of ardent anti-slavery and passionate pan-Africanism. Written in Chatham, Canada West, now Ontario, between 1856 and 1858, the novel began to appear in the New York-based *Anglo-African Magazine*, between January and July of 1859. The serialization was interrupted by Delany's expedition to Africa in May 1859, and not resumed, in the now *Weekly Anglo-African*, until December 1861, and concluding in early 1862. Delany (1812-1885) is a central figure in African-American literature, where he is credited as being an "early Afrocentric ideologue" (Austin 205) and as the fount of "an African-American literary river" (206). However, despite his three years in Canada West (where he relocated to flummox the evil US Fugitive Slave Act of 1850 and to promote a project of African-American emigration to either South America or Africa), and despite his authorship of *Blake* on Upper

Canadian soil, he has been granted no place in English-Canadian literary history. *Blake* is the third African-American novel, and so it is read in that culture as a response to US slavery and European imperialism in Africa. Yet, it may also be viewed as a radical, African-Canadian canvassing of the same concerns, one that could be read profitably in relation to George Brown's anti-slavery agitation in the Toronto *Globe* newspaper or even Susanna Moodie's settler memoir, *Roughing It in the Bush* (1852), which includes an account of the lynching of a black barber and cleaner, Tom Smith, somewhere in Canada West, for marrying an Irish woman (Moodie 211). Thus, *Blake* should be seen as an African-Canadian entry in an international debate over European imperialism and transatlantic slavery, whose North American resolution had national consequences for British North America. (Lest we forget, the military elimination of African servitude in the United States served as a stimulus to Canadian Confederation in 1867, thanks to the threat of armed, American revenge against British North America due to British imperial backing of the Dixie-States Confederacy during the US Civil War.)

Born in 1812 in Charles Town (West) Virginia, to a slave father and a free mother, Delany grew up with an intimate knowledge of his African roots, for "his Mandingo grandmother (who died at the age of 107)" used to "chant[] about her homeland," and his father was "the son of a Golah chieftain" (Takaki 83). Given his innate pride in his African ancestry as well as his failed bid for admission to Harvard Medical School, plus his scorn for slavery, Delany soon fixed upon black emigration as the appropriate reply to white oppression. Because blacks were a suppressed minority in the United States, they would have to relocate to exercise self-determination. Although Delany removed to Chatham, Canada West, in 1856, he considered Canada but a temporary haven. Even so, he was conscious of the impact of racism upon "coloured Canadians" and he excoriates white Canadian liberalism for its hypocritical attacks on American slavery, while condoning restrictions on Black Canadian education and economic opportunity. Hence, it is easy to place Delany's black nationalism and Pan-Africanism alongside the like ideologies of Philip (1947-) or the less definite, more playfully sinuous, mixed-race post-modernism of the poet Wayde Compton (1972-). Likewise, Delany's Byronic, revolutionary hero may be juxtaposed with Dionne

Brand's existentialist rebel heroines in her novel, *In Another Place, Not Here* (1996). Too Delany's polyphonic prose, akin to the "unique' ... argot formed of Latinate polysyllables, puns, translationese, stray associations, archaic English phraseology, and ... slang" (characteristics that Alan J. Peacock identifies in US poet Ezra Pound [Peacock 97]), is a style that many African-Canadian authors adopt.[x] So long as there are African-heritage Canadian writers, Delany will never truly die.

Delany differs from other early African/Black Canadian authors on the question of Christianity. Many passages in *Blake* complain about Caucasian Christian hypocrisy. Thus, Henry Blake asks, rhetorically, "What's religion to me? My wife is sold away from me by a man who is one of the leading members of the very church to which both she and I belong" (112). With deliberate irony, Henry later asserts, "Well, I'm a *runaway*, and from this time forth, I swear—I do it religiously—that I'll never serve any white man living!" (130). Writing to American abolitionist William Lloyd Garrison, on May 14, 1852, Delany favours, "Heathenism and Liberty, before Christianity and Slavery" (Takaki 94). For Delany, black liberation means building truly free black communities, not slavishly adopting "white" religion. Strains of this thought persist in Brand and Philip.

In contrast to Delany's reservations regarding "religion," Anglo-Christian attitudes determine the fiction of the first African-Canadian novelist native to British North America, namely, Amelia Etta Hall Johnson (1858-1922). Born to African-American parents in Canada West in 1858 and educated in Montreal, Johnson moved to Baltimore, Maryland, where, at age sixteen, she married the Rev. Harvey Johnson, D.D. In 1877, she began writing poems for what her biographer, I. Garland Penn, describes as "race periodicals" (Penn 422). Next, Johnson issued, in 1887, an "eight-page, monthly paper," *The Joy*, "containing original stories and poems" (422-424). Johnson's stories and poems also appeared in *The National Baptist*, "one of the largest circulated white denominational journals in the [US]" (424). Like Delany, who had written for Frederick Douglass's abolitionist newspaper, *The North Star*, from December 1847 to the summer of 1849, and who edited another

---

x   See my "Must All Blackness Be American?" (1996).

newspaper in 1875, Johnson became a "creative writer" after first playing the roles of editor and journalist. Penn delights to note that "in 1889-90 [Johnson] reached the place for which she had been aiming and preparing herself. She wrote for publication a manuscript, which was purchased by the American Baptist Publication Society, one of the largest publishing houses in America," thus making her "the first lady author whose manuscript has been accepted by this society" (424). Her next success is the "first Sunday-school library book written by a colored author" (425).

Indeed, Johnson's first novel, *Clarence and Corinne; or, God's Way*, published in Philadelphia in 1890 by the American Baptist Society, is— from a post-colonial and Afrocentric perspective—an oddity: All of her characters are white, or so the illustrations attest. Not only that, her novel is a Christian comedy: The saved lead blessed lives and, when troubles interrupt their not unpleasant progress, they rally, resituate themselves on the narrow path of righteousness, and achieve marriage, family unity, and due prosperity. Johnson's fiction reads like The Book of Job—if it were authored by Jane Austen. Introducing the 1988 reprint edition of *Clarence and Corinne*, African-American scholar Hortense Spillers confirms its status as "barely disguised tractarian writing. In other words, the narrative presses its polemical point by way of the story, which provides an occasion for the theme of social uplift" (xxvii). Moreover, "Nothing … earmarks this work specifically as one written by a 'black woman writer,' or an 'Afro-American,' and … there is very little or no evidence in the novel itself to suggest that Amelia E. Johnson wrote according to the putative urgencies of coeval black life in the United States" (xxvii). Sagely, Spillers advises that Johnson's decision to write fiction using only white characters reflects the feeling, as recorded by the African-American newspaper, the *Baptist Messenger*, that such writing, "is one of the silent, yet powerful agents at work to break down unreasonable prejudice, which is a hindrance to both races" (qtd in Spillers xxviii). By using white characters, Johnson hints that blacks rival whites in terms of writing and theology, psychology and insight. Thus, she calls racial categories into question at the historical moment when they are most rigid. Too, it is unlikely that the American Baptist Association could have—would have—published a Christian novel featuring boldly black characters. Accepting this reality, Spillers reclaims and redeems Johnson for African-

American literature by stating that "it is unimportant exactly *what* and *how* [Johnson] wrote, but altogether significant *that* she did" (xxviii). Certainly, "Her contemporaries saw the testimonial, exemplary force of her work as an instance of sociopolitical weaponry: 'the author of "Clarence and Corinne" feels confident that there are those among the race who need only to know that there is a way where there is a will, to follow her example, and *no doubt far surpass this, her first experience in bookmaking*; and she is happy in knowing that come what may, she has helped her people'" (Penn 426; emphasis mine)" (Spillers xxvii-xxix). In the novel, then, "race disappears ..., as human community loses specificity, except for its deeply embedded error" (xxx).

Yet, it is not an attempt to "smuggle in race"—as Spillers alleges that Johnson's readers do (xxxii)—to assert that a novel about poverty, familial *angst*, runaway fathers, and foster mothers refers to the legacy of slavery, just as it warns against the sins of city life. Thus, Clarence and Corinne live in a hovel resembling the slave shack of yore:

> Dismal as was the outside of this wretched abode, still more so was the inside. The floor, devoid of carpet, and unacquainted with soap and water, creaked underfoot, and in places was badly broken.
>
> The two or three rickety chairs, a rough pine table and crazy bedstead could hardly be dignified with the name of furniture. Some chipped plates and handleless cups were piled in confusion on the table ...
>
> A rickety stove, that was propped up on bricks, which did duty for legs, was littered with greasy pots and pans. Ashes strewed the hearth, and the few unbroken lights in the windows were so begrimed with dust as to be of little use, so far as letting in the daylight was concerned. (6)

To complete this slavery-like portrait, Johnson tells us that Clarence and Corinne were hovel "inmates" (6). Their mother is "the mistress of all this misery" (6) and upon her "countenance was stamped despair, and judging from her swollen eye, one also was the victim of ill-usage" (7). Now a shiftless husband hits her; formerly, a slave master or an overseer would have done so. When Clarence cries out, "Oh, how I wish we could dress decently, and go to school again like other children" (7), his plea for equality is not only a matter of class, but also of race, for segregation is pushing Southern blacks out of classrooms and back onto plantations, a regression enforced by Ku Klux Klan terrorism.

Clarence and Corinne is, then, like most Bible-based writing, an allegory—one that connects urban ills to moral lapses, yes, but also one that subtly reminds readers that the struggling, just-freed black men and women require social uplift as well as spiritual liberation. Thus, alcoholism replaces racism as the prime evil: The father of Clarence and Corinne is a mean drunk, and his violence and addiction kill his wife and disperse his children. The bottle stands in for the bullwhip; the inebriated daddy replaces the power-drunk "massa." Other aspects of slavery also appear. When Corinne has to reside with the miserly Miss Rachel Penrose, who believes "a bright fire … [is] a waste, and enough to eat entirely unnecessary" (Johnson 42), Corinne experiences "Nothing but hard work from morning until night" (47). One later learns that "The scanty food and poor clothing the child received was but little reward for the quantity of labor required of her" (68). "The poor little thing is overworked and underfed" (74). Moreover, like the archetypal, Gothic (and/or sadistic) slave masters, Miss Rachel, to establish Corinne's obedience to her severe economy and exacting standards, forces her to read only the Bible verses—"such as the twenty-eighth or twenty-ninth of Numbers, all about sacrifices, etc." (58), while ignoring "The beautiful stories of 'Joseph,' 'Daniel,' 'Samuel'" (58). Intriguingly, these latter stories supply the plots and imagery of many anti-slavery spirituals. Again, codedly, Johnson asks us to read the brutalizing effects of industrialization and urbanization, fuelled by lust, greed, and alcohol, as being akin to the degradations perpetrated by slavery.

I go further. *Clarence and Corinne* is domestic missionary work. Johnson seeks to truly "civilize" the United States. If the secret subject of the novel is the continuing damage wrought by now-abolished slavery upon American morale and social mores, its secret mission is to repair the Christian abolitionist alliance of blacks and whites, now sundered by post-Reconstruction politics. Perhaps its secret intertext is Harriet Beecher Stowe's Christian abolitionist novel, *Uncle Tom's Cabin, or Life Among the Lowly* (1852), which—radically—presents the slaves as *naturally* more moral than the slaveholding whites. Writing of black suffering *via* "whiteface," then, Johnson repeats Stowe's argument that redemption is available to all who struggle against evident immorality: Slave days then; slum life—with its vices—"now." From this perspective, *Uncle Tom's*—Christian—*Cabin* has been reduced to the alcoholic's shack in which Clarence and Corinne experience dispossession. Too, though their faces, illustrated, are white, their speech and subjects could come straight from Negro minstrelsy: "Yes'm," says Clarence (Johnson 11), among other locutions; and the "silk handkerchief" that he gives his sister is, in reality, "an old bandanna ... comically dilapidated" (10).

Though Johnson has been partially claimed by African-American scholarship, she belongs primordially to the African-Canadian canon. Moreover, her usage of white characters anticipates Suzette Mayr's fiction, more than a century later. In *The Widows* (1998), Mayr narrates the attempts of three elderly German women to baptize themselves into new lives by tumbling over Niagara Falls in a barrel. By succeeding, they also find redemption for the weight of the sufferings that their nation engendered by instigating the Second World War and committing crimes against humanity—including genocide. Championing elder empowerment, feminism, and lesbianism, the novel is also an oblique commentary on racial exclusion. In André Alexis's short fiction and novels, too, there is a tendency to deploy a multicultural and multiracial cast, ignoring *caste*, so that one must question just how much "colour" can be said to truly determine anyone's character.

Although James Madison Bell can be claimed for the African-Canadian canon, he was an African-American poet who worked as a plasterer in Canada West only from 1860 to 1865. Born in Ohio in 1826 and dying there in 1902, Bell has only a tenuous connection to African-Canadian and Canadian literature. He squeezes in references to Canada in "Modern Moses, or 'My Policy' Man," penned in the Confederation year of 1867, by mentioning "debauchees wherever found / from Baffin's Bay to Puget's Sound" (200). Yet, Bell's true subject is American politics.[xi]

Thus, let us consider the probable first collection of poems to be published by a born-in-Canada Black, namely, Robert Nathaniel Dett's *The Album of a Heart*, published in 1911 in Jackson, Tennessee. Raised in

---

xi   How does our understanding of the history of English-Canadian poetry shift if we include James Madison Bell as a "Confederation Poet"?

Drummondville—now Niagara Falls, Ontario, Dett (1882-1943) matters to African-American musicology, for, as a scholar of the Negro spiritual, he also compiled two essential texts: *Religious Folk-Songs of the Negro as Sung at Hampton Institute* (1927) and *The Dett Collection of Negro Spirituals* (1936). Importantly, Dett launches (or follows) several African-Canadian tendencies. *The Album of a Heart* utilizes both "dialect" as well as standard English—just as Black Canadian poets, novelists, and playwrights do today. The poem, "Conjured," is ragtime in rhythm:

> Couldn't sleep last night!
> Just toss and pitch!
> I'm conjured! I'm conjured!
> By that little witch!
>
> … Whenever I try to think;
> Side track and switch
> My thoughts do; and finally
> Dump me in the ditch. (46)

The diction is ragged too, more related to blues and the brothel than to the college where Dett was ensconced when his book was published. Yet, in the same volume as "Conjured," there is the stately, Tennysonian, "At Niagara," a fairly Victorian piece of *vers libéré*, or loosened blank verse:

> No! No! Not tonight, my Friend,
> I may not, cannot go with you tonight.
> And think not that I love you any less
> Because this now I'd rather be alone. (12)

The poem is rather mysterious; it could be about spiritual disaffection, homoerotic confusion, or suicidal brooding:

> Urge me no further, now that you understand.
> A nobler friend than you none ever knew
> But not this time. Tonight I'll be alone.… (13)

In "Pappy," Dett exploits the then-popular Plantation tradition in American poetry: "When I was a pickaninny / many years ago, / I members how my mammy used ter call me …" (Dett 1911, 19). One can almost imagine Al Jolson, in blackface, performing this "number." But, being Canadian, Dett produces, "Au Matin" (31)—a bit of Hardyesque drivel about ghostly dawns and gone love—and also "Au Soir" (32), which, being a better poem, syncopates copulation:

> Now does joy
> Its bounds transcend—
> Would the night
> Might never end!
> O soft shine on us
> From above,
> Beauteous Night
> Of perfect love. (33)

So, there you have it: The first published—at book-length—African-Canadian poet in English tosses out pop-song-styled lyrics, formal verse, alludes to French, and indulges in Dixie dialect. In addition, Dett was an expatriate intellectual, pursuing a career in the United States, presumably because there was no room in Canada—the Great White North—for a black man of his talents. A composer as well as a scholar, he remains a seminal Harlem Renaissance figure in the United States, but remembered here mainly in the prestigious, Toronto-based, eponymous Nathaniel Dett Chorale.[xii]

The first African-Canadian woman to issue a poetry collection was Anna Minerva Henderson (1887-1987), who was a retired civil servant, aged eighty, when her chapbook, *Citadel*, appeared in the Canadian Centennial year, in Saint John, New Brunswick. A New Brunswicker by birth, she is notable for having been a stellar pupil—really, an intellectual—in a time of few serious educational opportunities for blacks in general and black women in particular. Indeed, Henderson obtained a teacher's certificate, taught school in Nova Scotia, and then, in 1912, at age twenty-five, was hired into the federal civil service after writing an entrance test and earning *the third highest grade in the Dominion*. While in Ottawa, she wrote a column for the Ottawa Citizen titled "The Colyum" or "Just Among Ourselves" (Shadd 3). By the time she was fifty, Henderson

---

xii The Chorale's website provides a photograph of—and rightly laudatory bio for—Dett.

was publishing verse in little magazines. The bio note attending the publication of her sonnet, "Parliament Hill, Ottawa," in *Canadian Poetry Magazine* in 1937, allows only that she is unmarried ("Miss") and "a civil servant of Ottawa" ("News" 63). A year later, when this poem is reprinted in *New Harvesting: Contemporary Canadian Poetry, 1918-1938*, edited by Ethel Hume Bennett, the "Biographical Notes" remain magisterially laconic: "Anna M. Henderson, of Ottawa, has published verse in periodicals and magazines" (Bennett 194). When Henderson self-publishes *Citadel*, a slim booklet of thirty-one pages, she does not offer us either a "collected" or a "selected" poems. The latest dated poem in the book is from the winter of 1965 (Henderson 30) and the earliest (presumably) refers to 18 May 1947 (9). Yet, some of the poems appeared before 1947. This fact indicates that *Citadel* is a crafted chapbook focused on Saint John's cityscape and history, the British connection, faith, and the strife between artist and critic: it is neither a hodgepodge of musings nor a select batch of the author's "best." Rather, it is plainly her forceful entry into her city's literary culture, though few readers would have known she was black. Henderson inks sonnets and quatrains; hardly does *vers libre* darken her pages. She meditates on Loyalist history, the foggy look and soggy feel of Saint John, and, almost inaudibly, on race and racism. She sounds more like John Milton than she does Little Milton, for, likely, she wishes to prove—against racist and/or sexist naysayers—her (*race's*) competence in the field of letters. The key to Henderson's low-key style is "Mount Mansfield, Vermont": In this sonnet, the speaker exults in climbing the mountain—in a ski resort—and feels "singing happiness." Her exultation prefaces the claim, "This now we know— / That nevermore can level valley-ways / Shrouded in mist and sheltered far below, / Suffice to hold us captive through our days" (19). Superficially, the speaker is pleased to be at the summit of a redoubtable mountain, and feels that she may repeat the experience. But, in solid metaphysical tradition, Henderson moves the poem toward allegory: "And in the valley, dark in dreams below / Gleam here and there the twinkling lights of Stowe" (19). As it turns out, the Vermont resort is named after Stowe, whose *Uncle Tom's Cabin* (1852) served to ignite the US Civil War. Most subtly, Henderson is likening the mountain climb (prescient of Rev. Dr. Martin Luther King's imagery in his final sermon of April 3, 1968) to the dream of freedom once held by slaves, who looked to abolitionists like Stowe for inspiration. But the successful "escapee," now at the summit, basks in the moon's "floods of silver light" (19). A generation ago, a few Black Canadian critics chastised writer and playwright Alexis for not being, in essence, "black-identified enough" to merit their approval. Well, what will they do with Henderson, who made her singular poetry quite without any black support, but still found it possible to forward an African-Canadian voice, albeit in neoclassical registers?

The first African/Black Canadian to publish a play in English achieved that distinction only in 1965, but the circumstances were auspicious: Lennox John Brown (1934-), a native of Trinidad, won a competition, then run annually by the Ottawa Little Theatre, in Ottawa, Ontario, to seek out and publish the best "new" Anglo-Canadian plays. (If one counts Fouché's pre-emigration publications in Haiti, then he is the first Black Canadian to publish a play in French. I refer here to *Un fauteuil dans un crâne* [1957].[xiii]) Brown was only in Canada a decade or so before moving on to the United States, although his later biography is skeletal-sketchy. What can be said is that *The Captive* (1965) was issued not as a book, but rather as a bound typescript, fifty-seven pages in length. Notably, Brown, being an Afro-Caribbean immigrant to—or long-term resident in—Canada sees, as "early" as 1965, that African Canadians are superbly variegated, so that prospects for unified action are slim. His *dramatis personae* includes Clarence—"a Negro medical student from Jamaica" (Brown "The Captive," 1); Oseka—"an African student from Kenya" (1); Jimmy—"a Negro from Harlem" (1); and Norm—"a Canadian Negro" (11). These four black men have kidnapped a white man, an anonymous southerner from the US who has been trying to organize a Canadian chapter of the Ku Klux Klan. Though they violate the liberty and life of another human being, the black men's unity in this gangster undertaking suggests, ironically, positive possibilities for concerted, joint political alliance throughout the African Diaspora. But Brown's elaboration of the men's backgrounds soon shows their unity to be paper-thin. "JIMMY, the Harlemite, is tense, lithe and athletic.... [He] is essentially a man of action ..." (4). "OSEKA ... is cool,

---

xiii If one accepts my arguments, Fouché published both the first African/Black Canadian book of poetry *and* the first African/Black Canadian play in French, both in Haiti. This fact should make him a Francophone African-Canadian writer that we must study.

businesslike and efficient. He is that dangerous combination of thought and action" (4). "CLARENCE ... is a dreamer. He has an indecisive passive quality that suggests weakness" (4). "NORM"—tellingly the born Black Canadian—is not a student, but a "railway porter" (11), who "*appears* to be an outgoing type who laughs easily" (11, my emphasis), and, who, when we first see him, has been "drinking and is a bit tipsy" (11). Like Jimmy, he is "mercurial" and can be "quite violent—even to the people closest to them" (11). Brown's portraiture is both clichéd and complex. The two working-class types are American and Canadian, but the latter is more degraded, presumably because he has no political and economic power (unlike Oseka and Clarence) and no cultural influence (unlike Jimmy). Oseka and Clarence, one African and the other Caribbean, are either middle-class already or middle-class in aspiration. They are not the sons of disempowered minorities, but representatives of new nations, just freed from Caucasian-shaded imperialism. That these four should unite to terrorize a supposed member of a white terrorist organization *could* be read as propagandistic posturing. But Brown complicates—no, negates—this possibility by, first, showing that Oseka and Clarence are rivals for the affections of "JOAN ... an unusually attractive white girl of about 22. Her long blonde hair and fair skin give her a fairy-like impression" (25). Her brother, John, also a character, is a liberal white who befriends the Negroes. Shortly, the kidnapped man dies, and his captors are wracked by guilt—and fear of the noose (capital punishment is operative in Canada in 1965); Joan and John are torn by what to say to the police, if they dast say anything; and Oseka admits his love for Joan, who—sorrowfully for him—reaffirms her love for Clarence. The play is sharply written and the lines attain a prose poetry that lifts it high above the Civil Rights Movement events that may have inspired its development. Brown's characters are compelling, though the playwright seems most dismissive of Norm as the Black Canadian drunkard—a symbol of black failure whereas Jimmy exemplifies black struggle. This portraiture—caricature—is affirmed by Brown's 1972 statement, "there is no substantial Black culture in Canada" (Brown, "A Crisis" 8).

Brown's peremptorily dismissive comment—and the echoing iterations of it by many scholars since—requires precisely this volume that you will soon read as its corrective. This too-brief anthology, *Locating Home*, registers, via the reproduction of the substantive texts of Johnson, Dett, and Henderson, the indelible fact of the existence of "substantial Black" *cultures*—plural—in Canada, for these cultures are variegated due to different periods of incoming-black arrival in disparate parts of the *evolving* state under very distinctive (and often regionally inflected) protocols. We must suspend the notion that there is a monolithic "Black culture" in Canada that is identifiably the *same* as forms of African Diasporic identity observable elsewhere. By bothering to recuperate—scrupulously—the conjures (creative writings) and critiques of the early or the "first" African-Canadian scribes, we begin to glimpse the existence of this Nordic form of African-heritage expressivity—even if the original authors are themselves yet unconscious of the (incipient group) identity. *Locating Home* is a step in this direction, though a national, bilingual anthology will be necessary—as soon as possible—if we should like to perceive, more comprehensively, the imperatives of African-Canadian literature from its inception. Theoretically, at least, the establishment of an—or "the"—archive of African-Canadian literature will make discussion of even current texts more coherent, if not "literate."

I hereby remind myself, dear reader, that the purpose of an anthology (or a bibliography) is to marshal evidence—proof—of the existence of a canon that *has always been*, but, simultaneously, has always been overlooked. Yet, as soon as the anthologist or bibliographer compiles or selects this *provisional* canon, he or she exposes it to potentially fatal interrogation of its worth. Once such a body of texts has achieved "the light of day," must anyone give it "the time of day"? It is in answering this interrogative that the anthologist or bibliographer proves his or her acumen, mettle, and, to cite Chandler again, "authority." It is his or her editing, his or her selection or compilation of texts, that secures their canonical value—or *not*. Too, in positing the merits of discrete texts and authors, the anthologist or bibliographer challenges the borders or margins of other canons, other schools, affirming that canonical status, of whatever form, is not fixed, but open-ended. If the anthologist—or bibliographer—puts a set of texts and scribes on public trial, let's imagine, his or her selection or compilation is itself proof of the subjects' inherent canonicity.

Dear reader, I now request that the affectionate assemblage of early African-Canadian literature continue apace with *you*. *Locating Home* is only a jumping-off point—a catalyst, a provocation, not a conclusion. Gifted with unlimited resources, I'd've included the texts of Brown, Fouché, Delany, and yet others. However, I do plead that Johnson, Dett, and Henderson yield a fine entrée into African-Canadian literature, which is not embryonic in their case, but fully formed, inaugurating recurrent themes and poetics. Consider this trio of texts, then, as already constitutive and definitive of African-Canadian literature, with requisite pulse, breath, nervous system, memory, vision, already mature, already operative …

Works Cited

Austin, Allan D. "Delany, Martin R." *The Oxford Companion to African American Literature*. New York: Oxford University Press, 1997. 205-206.

Badaracco, Claire Hoertz. *Trading Words: Poetry, Typography, and Illustrated Books in the Modern Literary Economy*. Baltimore: The Johns Hopkins University Press, 1995.

Bell, James Madison. "Modern Moses, or 'My Policy' Man." In *African-American Poetry of the Nineteenth Century: An Anthology*. Ed. Joan R. Sherman. Urbana: University of Illinois Press, 1992. 199-209.

Bennett, Ethel Hume. "Biographical Notes." In *New Harvesting: Contemporary Canadian Poetry, 1918-1938*, ed. Ethel Hume Bennett. Toronto: Macmillan, 1938. 193-198.

Canadian Poetry Magazine. "News Notes of Contributors." 2.1 (June 1937): 63.

Brand, Dionne. *In Another Place, Not Here*. Toronto: Alfred A. Knopf Canada, 1996.

Brown, John Lennox. "The Captive: Snow Dark Sunday." *Ottawa Little Theatre*, Ranking Play Series 2, Catalogue No. 43, September 1965.

-----. "A Crisis: Black Culture in Canada." *Black Images*. 1.1 (Jan. 1972): 4-8.

Chandler, Nahum Dimitri. "The Economy of Desedimentation: W.E.B. DuBois and the Discourses of the Negro." *Callaloo*. 19.1 (Winter 1996): 78-93.

Clarke, George Elliott. "Must All Blackness be American? Locating Canada in Borden's "Tightrope Time," or Nationalizing Gilroy's *The Black Atlantic*." *Canadian Ethnic Studies*. 28.3 (1996): 56-71.

-----. *Odysseys Home: Mapping African-Canadian Literature*. Toronto: University of Toronto Press, 2002.

-----. "Toward Establishing an—or the—'Archive' of African Canadian Literature." *Editing as Cultural Practice in Canada*. Eds. Dean Irvine and Smaro Kamboureli. Waterloo (ON): Wilfrid Laurier University Press, 2016. 41-56.

Delany, Martin Robison. *Blake; or, The Huts of America*. 1859; 1861-1862. Rpt. *Violence in the Black Imagination: Essays and Documents*. Ed. Ronald T. Takaki. 1972. Expanded Edition. New York: Oxford University Press, 1993. 102-214.

Dett, Robert Nathaniel. *The Album of a Heart*. Jackson, TN: Mocowat-Mercer / Lane College, 1911.

-----. *Religious Folk-Songs of the Negro As Sung at Hampton Institute*. Hampton, VA: Hampton Institute Press, 1927.

-----. *The Dett Collection of Negro Spirituals*. N.P.: Hall and McCrealy, 1936.

Dionne, René. *La Littérature régionale aux confins de l'histoire at de la géographie: Étude*. Sudbury, ON: Prise de parole, 1993.

Foucault, Michel. 1992. *Language, Counter-Memory, Practice: Selected Essays and Interviews*. Donald F. Bouchard. Trans. Donald F. Bouchard and Sherry Simon. 1977. Ithaca, NY: Cornell University Press, 1992.

Fouché, Franck. *Un fauteuil dans un crâne*. In *Optique*. Haiti, 1957.

-----. *Message*. Port-au-Prince: Nemours Telhomme, 1946.

Henderson, Anna Minerva. Parliament Hill, Ottawa. *Canadian Poetry Magazine* 2.1 (June 1937): 51.

-----. Parliament Hill, Ottawa. In *New Harvesting: Contemporary Canadian Poetry, 1918-1938*, ed. Ethel Hume Bennett. Toronto: Macmillan, 1938. 54.

-----. *Citadel*. Fredericton: Henderson, 1967.

Johnson, Amelia Etta Hall. *Clarence and Corinne; or, God's Way*. 1890. New York: Oxford University Press, 1988.

Kamboureli, Smaro. Introduction. *Making a Difference: Canadian Multicultural Literature*. Ed. Smaro Kamboureli. Toronto: Oxford University Press, 1996. 1-16.

Korn, Marianne. "Preface: Ezra Pound and History." *Ezra Pound and History*. Ed. Marianne Korn. Orono, ME: National Poetry Foundation, 1985. [7]-[11].

Mayr, Suzette. *The Widows*. Edmonton: NeWest Press, 1998.

Moodie, Susanna. *Roughing It in the Bush: Or, Life in Canada*. 1852. Toronto: McClelland & Stewart, 1989.

Nathaniel Dett Chorale. Website. http://nathanieldettchorale.org/about/roots/. Accessed October 17, 2011.

Peacock, Alan J. "Pound and Propertius: The Limitations of an Historical Persona." *Ezra Pound and History*. Ed. Marianne Korn. Orono, ME: National Poetry Foundation, 1985. 83-98.

Penn, I. Garland. *The Afro-American Press and Its Editors*. 1891. New York: Arno Press and the New York Times, 1969.

Philip, M. NourbeSe. *Frontiers: Selected Essays and Writings on Racism and Culture, 1984—1992*. Stratford, ON: 1992.

-----. *A Genealogy of Resistance and Other Essays*. Toronto: Mercury, 1997.

Shadd, Adrienne. Memory, Race and Silence: The Poetry of Anna Minerva Henderson (1887-1987). 1996. TS in the possession of the author.

Sher, Richard. "The Book in the Scottish Enlightenment." *The Culture of the Book in the Scottish Enlightenment*. Ed. Paul Wood. Toronto: Thomas Fisher Rare Book Library, 2000. 40-60.

Schultz, Kathy Lou. *The Afro-Modernist Epic and Literary History: Tolson, Hughes, Baraka*. New York: Palgrave-Macmillan, 2013. Print.

Spillers, Hortense. Introduction. *Clarence and Corinne; or, God's Way*. By Mrs. A. E. Johnson. 1890. New York: Oxford University Press, 1988. xxvii-xxxviii.

Stowe, Harriet Beecher. *Uncle Tom's Cabin, or Life Among the Lowly*. 1852. New York: Modern, 1948.

Takaki, Ronald T. *Violence in the Black Imagination: Essays and Documents*. New York: G.P. Putnam's Sons, 1972.

Walcott, Rinaldo. *Black Like Who?* Toronto: Insomniac Press, 1997.

White, Hayden. *Tropics of Discourse: Essays in Cultural Criticism*. 1978. Baltimore: The Johns Hopkins University Press, 1985.

X, Malcolm, and Alex Haley. *The Autobiography of Malcolm X*. New York: Random House, 1965.

Clarence and Corinne

Amelia Etta Hall Johnson

CHAPTER I

Discouraged

Breaking down of nuclear family structure
No family = apocalyptic surroundings

On the outskirts of the pretty town of N———, among neat vine-covered homes, like a blot upon a beautiful picture, there stood a weather-beaten, tumble down cottage.

Its windows possessed but few unbroken panes, and rags took the place of glass. The rough door hung on a single hinge, which was so rusty as almost to refuse to perform its duty for the paintless boards that hung upon it for support. There was a little garden plot in front, separated from the street by broken palings, and a gate that was never closed. The brick walk that led to the house was uneven and grass-grown; while weeds grew unmolested in the hard, dry soil which had been intended for fairer and more fragrant occupants.

Dismal as was the outside of this wretched abode, still more so was the inside. The floor, devoid of carpet, and unacquainted with soap and water, creaked under foot, and in places was badly broken.

The two or three rickety chairs, a rough pine table and crazy bedstead could hardly be dignified with the name of furniture. Some chipped plates and handleless cups were piled in confusion on the table, and had evidently been left there since noon. *Intention*

A rickety stove, that was propped up on bricks, which did duty for legs, was littered with greasy pots and pans. Ashes strewed the hearth, and the few unbroken lights in the windows were so begrimed with dust as to be of little use, so far as letting in the daylight was concerned. *Contradiction*

So much for the dwelling; now for the inmates. *Apothecaries?*

In an old rocking chair sat the mistress of all this misery. In her hands she held a tattered garment, bearing but small semblance to either male or female attire. She had been engaged, apparently, in attempting to draw together some of the many rents into which it had been torn; but whether the task had seemed a hopeless one, or whether her thoughts were far away from her occupation, I cannot say. At any rate, her hands were resting listlessly in her lap, where they had dropped, with the work still unfinished between her fingers.

Aside from the fact that her appearance partook of the general aspect of her surroundings, she was a comely woman, but one upon whose countenance was stamped despair, and, judging from her swollen eye, one also who was the victim of ill-usage.

She was the sole occupant of the room at the time our story opens, but she did not remain so long, for presently the half-open door was pushed back on its unwilling hinge, and a boy of twelve years entered, followed by a little girl of nine. They were both attractive children, notwithstanding the fact that they bore in their appearance and faces the stamp of neglect and scanty fare.

The boy advanced to his mother's side, and throwing himself down on the floor, resting his elbow on her knee and his head upon his hand, burst out impetuously: "Oh, how I wish we could dress decently, and go to school again like other children!"

The mother roused herself from her apathy and looked at him, half curiously, half sadly.

"What now, Clarence? What's the good of wishing for what can't be?" she said, wearily.

"But why can't it be? It drives me just wild to see the boys coming from school, and to know that they have been there learning, while we're just running around every day; and I'm getting so big too. Now, there's Tom and Lizzie Green; we met them to-day going to school, looking decent and clean, and, of course, Mr. Tom had to holler 'ragamuffin' at me; but I didn't give it to him, did I?" And the boy chuckled with satisfaction at the way he had served his tormentor.

"Yes; but, Clarence, I was really sorry for poor Lizzie, she was so frightened; besides, I like her: she don't call names, and always speaks to me."

This came from Corinne, Clarence's sister, who had seated

herself on the edge of the ragged bed.

"Come, come, my boy," said Mrs. Burton, taking up her mending again, in a disheartened way, and beginning to draw the needle and thread slowly back and forth.

"There's no use talking, and there's no use trying to be decent when your father is likely to come home drunk at any time, and knock and beat a body about as he does. I tell you it's no use talking." And her voice rang out sharp and harsh. "Take the basket," she continued, after a moment's pause, "and go and get some chips to start a fire to get some supper, if your father should bring anything home to eat."

Silenced, but not satisfied, the boy obeyed and left the room, followed closely by his sister. He knew that what his mother said was true, and he felt that there was but little benefit to be gained by talking.

Corinne was devotedly fond of her brother, whom she considered a miracle of wisdom; and indeed the lad did have a fund of information about things in general, acquired after the manner usual to observant boys. To this was added an ardent desire to possess an education. Then he was honest and truthful; in fact, he was a boy who might become a useful man; but, as he said to his sister, as he walked slowly along, "he'd no chance."

"Corrie," he exclaimed, suddenly coming to a stand-still, and flinging the old basket away from him savagely, "I'm going to run away; so there, now!"

The little girl looked at him in amazement, for a moment, too surprised to say anything. Then the tears gathered in her black eyes, and she said, reproachfully:

"Oh Clarence! Will you go away and leave me?"

The boy was not proof against the pleading look in the sad little face, for if there was one person in the world whom he really loved, it was his sister. And now, as he looked at her, the fierce hard look slowly died out of his face.

"Now that's just it, Corinne," he said, "if it wasn't for you, I'd go to-morrow; but I do hate to leave you. Never mind, don't cry; maybe something will turn up some day. Here, wipe your eyes on my silk handkerchief."

This had the effect he desired on the little girl, for a smile spread over her face, like sunshine after rain, and she laughed merrily; for the "silk handkerchief" of which her brother spoke was an old bandanna which was so comically dilapidated as to make it a matter of doubt as to whether she would find sufficient handkerchief with which to dry her tears.

While the children were thus engaged with each other a lady approached. The boy and his sister moved aside so that she might pass; but instead of doing this, she came to a stop in front of them.

They looked up into her face in surprise. A very pleasant face it was that they saw, lighted by a pair of very dark and very bright eyes. Clarence knew the face; it was that of a teacher in the school, the very same school that he was so anxious to attend. Yes, he knew her well enough, for he had met her often, and once or twice she had smiled at him, but had never spoken before.

"Your name is Clarence Burton, is it not?" she asked, pleasantly, after surveying the boy from head to foot.

"Yes'm," he answered, looking down at the ground.

"And is the little girl your sister?"

"Yes'm," he said again, "she's Corrie."

"Well, Clarence, why don't you and Corrie come to school?'

"I've nothing fit to come in; neither has Corrie."

"But you would like to come, wouldn't you?"

"Yes ma'am; it's what I'd like to do more'n anything."

"Won't your mother let you come?"

"Don't know as she'd care, but we ain't going anywhere to be called names, we ain't." And the old hard look came again into the boy's eyes, and he picked up his basket, and was moving away unceremoniously. But it wasn't a part of Miss Gray's plan to have him go yet.

"Clarence," she said, "don't you know that it isn't just polite to do that?"

Something in her voice made Clarence halt, in spite of himself, although he felt as if he would like very much to run away as fast as he could.

He looked up again in the lady's face, expecting to see the "school ma'am" in it, but there was the same kindly expression in the dark eyes that he had seen before.

Again he dropped his to the ground, and twisted a bit of the poor ill-used basket between his uneasy fingers, but he said not a word.

"Clarence", began Miss Gray again, "I have been noticing you for a long time, and I have passed by your home a great many times; and, my poor boy, I know all about it and I'm so sorry for you." And she reached out her neatly gloved hand and took the boy's grimy one and gave it a squeeze.

This was altogether more than Clarence could stand, especially in his present state of mind, and he snatched his hand away and hid his face with it. Of course, he wouldn't have anyone think that he was crying—oh, no, not for a moment; but however that may be, there was a tremulousness in his voice when he answered Miss Gray's kind "good-bye." "I'm coming to see your mother soon, Clarence," she added, with a parting smile at Corinne, who had done nothing but gaze at the pleasant face of their new acquaintance.

The children watched her for a while after she left them, and then they slowly turned and resumed their interrupted walk. They were going to a new house that was being built, some blocks distant from their home.

Not one word did either of them say until they had reached the building, and were busily engaged in filling their basket with the bits of wood and shavings that had been left by the workmen.

When the basket would hold no more they sat down to rest.

"Clarence," said Corinne, looking about her, curiously, "who do you s'pose will live in this house when it's finished?"

"How should I know," returned her brother, rather tartly.

"It's going to be a nice house, Clarence," she went on, without heeding the curtness of the answer to her former question, "and I guess the people that'll live in it will have all sorts of nice things. It must be fine to have all the nice things you want." And the little girl sighed wistfully, as she thought how barren of "nice things" her own poor little life was.

"Don't you fret, Corrie," said her brother, comfortingly; "one of these days you shall have nice things too."

"Where will they come from, Clarence?" asked the child, opening her brown eyes wide.

"Oh, you'll see," was Clarence's answer, given with a wise shake of the head, as he arose to go; and bidding Corinne "come on," he added that the new house was nothing to them, "and never would be." Ah, Clarence, how little we know what the future contains for us!

CHAPTER II

A Grim Visitor

By the time the children reached home it was dark. No light, however, shone through the dingy windows of the cottage. The boy pushed open the door, and entered, with his sister close behind him.

They found their mother still seated in the old chair, but she was now rocking herself back and forth, her face hidden in her hands, and crying bitterly, but softly.

"What is it, mother?" asked Clarence, anxiously, coming to her side. "What is the matter?"

For answer, his mother pointed to the miserable bed in the corner, upon which was stretched the form of a man.

The boy understood all now. It was no new thing for him to come home and find his mother sobbing over some fresh ill-treatment inflicted upon her by her drink-maddened husband.

For a moment, all was still, save for the heavy breathing of the sleeping man. Then the wretched woman arose, and going noiselessly to the cupboard, took from it two pieces of bread, and putting them into the hands of the two children, motioned them to go to bed. Silently, they obeyed, for upon silence depended their chances of a quiet night. Had they been so unfortunate as to waken the figure upon the bed, a torrent of abuse would have been theirs: so they were only too glad to creep off to their beds — Corinne to her pallet on the floor of the room in which they were, and Clarence to his in their bare attic. Then their mother resumed her old position, but she was quiet now.

Poor little Corinne, too wretched to eat, lay quietly in her corner, with the great tears chasing each other down her thin cheeks, until at length she lost sight of her misery in the sound sleep of childhood.

Clarence, in his hard, comfortless bed, was inwardly chafing at his lot; his heart was full of bitter, bitter thoughts against everybody and everything. It was long before he slept.

The night wore away and day dawned. The sunbeams struggled to peep in at the dirty windows of the cottage, but with poor success. They did manage, however, to flit for an instant across the face of sleeping Corinne. Perhaps it was this that awakened her; at any rate, waken she did, and, raising herself on her elbow, looked about for her mother. To her surprise, she saw her sitting in the same position in which she had last seen her the evening before. The father was still sleeping on the bed, across which he had thrown himself, hats, boots, and all.

Corinne arose softly, and crept to her mother's side. She had no dressing to do, for she had laid herself down just as she was. Thinking her mother asleep, she stretched out her hand to touch her.

Why did she start back in alarm? Why, indeed? Those dull eyes that stared at her from that stony face plainly told her, child though she was, that her mother was dead. With a wild, frightened cry, she sprang toward the bed where her father lay, and in her terror losing sight of her fear of him, she frantically shook the sleeping man, crying, "Oh, father, father, wake up; do wake up; mother is dead! Oh, what shall I do?"

With an oath her father rolled over, and raising his clenched hand aimed a blow at his child; but Corinne dodged his upraised fist, at the same time continuing her cry.

At length the fact slowly dawned upon the man's beclouded brain that something out of the common had occurred. He raised himself, and after gazing about him stupidly for a while, arose and walked unsteadily to his wife's side.

Once in front of those wide-open eyes, all apathy disappeared, and he seized her by the shoulder and shook her, calling to her to "Wake up!" But the poor broken-spirited, abused woman was sleeping her last sleep; she would wake up no more in this world.

"Oh, father, mother is dead; what made her die?" moaned Corinne.

"I dunno," was the answer. Then hurriedly bidding her call her brother, the hard hearted father left the house and hastened away, no one knew wither, leaving the two children all alone with the dead.

Just as the door closed, Clarence came down.

"What is the matter, Corrie?" he asked, seeing his sister sobbing so bitterly.

"Oh, Clarence, just look: poor, poor mother is dead."

"Dead? Mother dead?" ejaculated the boy, in a dazed way, slowly advancing toward the motionless figure. He lifted one of the nerveless hands, only to let it drop with a shiver as its cold touch met his. For a moment he was silent; then he murmured, half absently, "Yes, dead. Poor mother!"

"Oh, Clarence!" wailed poor Corrie, pressing close to her brother's side. The boy put his arm around the trembling little figure. Poor child! she was so nervous; such a tender little plant! People used to wonder why she was so different from the rest of the family. The father, rough, uncouth, and almost always under the influence of liquor. The mother, careless and unkempt. Clarence, rugged and impetuous, but thoroughly good-natured. Corinne both looked and was different from these, and had always been so.

"Clarence, why did mother die?" sobbed the child.

"Why did she die?" repeated the boy, vehemently.

"How could she live, battered and beaten, and starved as she was, and by our father too; the one who could have made us all comfortable and happy. But instead of that he's made us miserable — no, it wasn't him, either; it was that dreadful, dreadful stuff, whisky. Yes, drink ruined our father, and now it's killed our mother; and nobody cares for us because we're the children of a drunkard. People don't even want to give me work because of it; and they call me 'old drunken Burton's boy.'"

"Oh, don't, don't talk so; you frighten me," cried Corinne, clinging closer to her brother than ever.

The boy, relieved by having given vent to some of the bitterness that had been pent up in his bosom for so long, now burst into tears, and the brother and sister wept together until they were aroused by a rap on the door.

It was one of the neighbors, who said that their father had stopped at her door and told her that there was something the matter with his "old woman," and had asked her to come and see what it was. Not knowing what had happened, Mrs. Greene had not hurried, having stayed to attend to some of her own household affairs.

Great was her astonishment and deep her indignation when she found how matters stood at the cottage; and she was loud in her denunciations of "that heartless Jim Burton." "No wonder he was moving off so fast, he's likely to be took up for murder. If he ain't killed that poor woman outright, he's done it by inches. But come, chicks, cheer up; don't take on so. Run over to my house while I fix up here a bit, and tell my Tom you're to have your breakfast." And the kind-hearted woman began turning about to see what she should do first. To her surprise, the boy quietly, but firmly said: "Mrs. Greene, I'd rather not go to your house."

"Why not?" she asked.

"I'd rather not go," he repeated. "I don't want any breakfast."

"Oh, well, of course you needn't go if you don't want to, but you ought to have something to eat. But never mind; I'm going up street a minute or so, and I'll bring you something." And away went Mrs. Greene, spreading, as she went, the news that "Jim Burton's wife had died sudden."

The coroner was notified, and of course there was an inquest, and a verdict rendered that "death was caused by heart trouble," which was true enough, in more senses than one.

But to go back to the children: True to her promise, Mrs. Greene brought with her some breakfast, which she pressed Clarence and Corinne to eat. The worthy woman had attributed the boy's reluctance to visit her house to a backwardness on his part, but in reality it was due to the fact that it was the home of Tom Greene. He was poor, wretchedly poor and forlorn, but he was proud. He saw in Tom Greene the only boy who delighted in tormenting him, and calling him and his sister names.

Mrs. Greene had also brought with her a tall, spare, hard-featured personage, whom she addressed as "Miss Rachel Penrose," who it seemed was the owner of the old cottage and the ground upon which it stood. A woman of few words was Miss Rachel; one who was "willing to do her duty," as she expressed it, but it was done much after the manner of Pharisees: her deeds were done to be seen by men. A woman of another stamp was her companion, simple-hearted Mrs. Greene, who was ever ready, from pure sympathy, to lend a hand wherever it was needed; and it was sadly needed here, in this abode of wretchedness and death. She now urged the children to eat, but neither of them was inclined to do so. The boy "wasn't hungry," and his sister was too full of her trouble, so the food was set away untasted.

The coroner had come and gone, so too had the crowd of curious sight-seers; then the task of "cleaning up," which was by no means an easy one, was begun; and Miss Rachel could not forbear remarking in an undertone that it was a mystery to her "how people could be so shiftless," further asserting that to her mind "Mrs. Burton didn't amount to much."

"Ah, Miss Rachel, but you must think of what the poor creature had to put up with! What with Burton's drinkin' and abuse, you wouldn't have much heart to keep things nice if you were starved and knocked about like she was."

Mrs. Greene's defense of the unfortunate woman had but little effect by way of softening her hearer.

"Why didn't she work and keep herself from starving; I'm sure I'd a great sight rather do that and keep myself and children decent, than to give way and just sit down with my hands in my lap and let everything get topsy-turvy."

Miss Rachel's hands were by no means idle while her tongue was busy. Things were getting in pretty good shape under her methodical touch and Mrs. Greene's energetic efforts.

The two forlorn children sat together near the window, in the old rocking chair, too deeply absorbed in their own sorrowful thoughts to heed what was going on around them.

The old bed had been made tidy from good Mrs. Greene's scanty store of bed linen, and the body of the dead woman, neatly arrayed by the same kind hands, was lying peacefully upon it. Nobody knew much about the Burtons, for they talked to no one. All that was known about them was that they had come to the little cottage one day, with their few belongings, but from whence no one knew. Mrs. Burton was neat and respectable looking then; so were her children, who were quite small.

At first, the place was kept as neat as possible, but not long; for as the husband and father grew more and more intemperate, the wife and mother grew disheartened and careless. Then, too, the children had been sent to school, but it had now been a long time since they had gone.

Clarence was not an idle boy by nature, and he had tried to get work, and did work when he could get it to do; but with all his poverty he was very proud, and could not brook the sneers and taunts of those with whom he came in contact; so he was not very fortunate in finding employment. And just as often as not, when he had earned a little money, his father had taken it from him to spend in drink.

Things were in this condition when the grim visitor—"Death"— stepped in and removed the mother.

She had lived a hopeless life, and no one knew otherwise than that she had died a hopeless death. She had gone without a word, and none save God knew aught of her last moments.

CHAPTER III
Friends

The long night passed slowly away in the little cottage. Mrs. Greene, the only person, except Miss Rachel Penrose, who had come near the children since their bereavement, for anything more than curiosity, stayed with them. They had both slept a little but the night had seemed very dreary, and they were glad when morning dawned. Their mother was to be buried that day by the town, for their father had gone away, no one knew where. He had not been seen since he left the cottage the morning before, save by Mrs. Greene, with whom he had exchanged a few words, asking her to go over and see what ailed his wife.

About six o'clock, the kind neighbor left them for a while, to go to her home in order to prepare breakfast for her family. Thinking that Clarence and Corinne would be more likely to eat something if Lizzie carried it to them, she accordingly sent the little girl over with some coffee and toast. She thought rightly, for the shy ways and sympathizing words of the child won the brother and sister from their lonely sorrow, and she succeeded in coaxing them to eat a little of the toast and drink the coffee.

Mrs. Greene entered while the three sat quietly talking together. She brought with her a suit of clothes for Clarence and a dress for Corinne, so that they might follow their mother to her grave, looking at least respectable. The clothes, she thought, would do nicely, for Tom and Clarence were about the same size, and Lizzie was very little larger than Corinne.

The two little girls parted reluctantly, but were pleased when they were told that Corinne should come and stay with Lizzie after the funeral. As Lizzie Greene passed out at the gate, she met Miss Gray just going in. Remembering her promise to Clarence, she had determined to stop at the cottage, on her way to school, and have a talk with Mrs. Burton. With a smile to Lizzie, she walked up the uneven path and tapped lightly on the door. It was not until she had rapped that she noticed the crape upon it.

Clarence, who from the window had caught a glimpse of his new friend, hastened to meet her. All unprepared for the sad scene that met her gaze, she exclaimed: "Why, Clarence! What does this mean?"

"Mother died night before last, ma'am," explained the boy, as steadily as he could, while Corinne only sobbed.

"Yes, miss," volunteered Mrs. Greene, coming forward; "she died quite suddenly. Nobody knows how, nor just when."

"Poor children!" murmured Miss Gray. Then addressing the friendly neighbor, she asked: "Where is her husband?"

"That's what none of us can tell, miss. He took himself off as soon as it happened."

"And left these children here all alone?"

"That's what he did, miss."

"Poor things!" And the visitor sat down, and drawing the weeping Corinne to her, gently soothed her, while the boy told all he knew of the sad story.

The young school teacher stayed as long as she could with the lonely children, and when she left at last it seemed to them as if she had taken a part of the sunshine with her. Miss Gray was full of sympathy for her little friends, and as she walked along her thoughts were busy trying to devise some way in which to help them. They were in her thoughts all day, and when school was over, and she turned her steps homeward, she was still thinking of them. It was a beautiful afternoon in June. The sun was shining brightly upon the flowers in the tasteful gardens in front of the pretty homes that lined the quiet streets through which she passed. Here and there, a gay butterfly fluttered, or a busy bee flitted from blossom to blossom.

"The world seems very lovely and peaceful this afternoon." thought the young girl, as she paused before the gate of her own little home. She lifted the latch and walked slowly up the neatly kept walk to the house.

The home of Helen Gray was a small but picturesque white cottage, over whose porch clambered roses and honeysuckle, and in whose garden bloomed many a bright blossom. Inside, the little house was as neat, cool, and cosy as the hands of Mary, Helen's younger sister, could make it. Mary was an invalid. She had been frail and sickly from a little child. She was therefore unable to mingle with the busy world, but did her very best to make home pleasant for her beloved sister. Although she was not given to repining, — her disposition was altogether too sweet and gentle for that, — she could not help fretting sometimes because she could not go out and work, and earn money too. But Helen would always say: "No, no, dear. Let me do the going, and you the staying. I couldn't do both, you know." And then she would laugh merrily, but would add, more soberly: "What would I do if I had no Mary to keep house for me, and to talk to me when I come home? You are a very important personage, Miss Mary, and you must endure your importance as best you can."

The two sisters lived all alone, the elder supporting both by her teaching. They were orphans, and were strongly attached to each other.

On this afternoon, Mary was sitting by the open window sewing, ever and anon looking up to admire the bright picture without, and to enjoy the perfume of the flowers, as the soft breeze wafted it to her. A smile stole over her thin face as she saw her sister approaching. An answering smile lit up the features of Helen as she came to the invalid's side, and stooped and kissed the upturned lips. Then removing her hat, she seated herself in a low rocking chair, exclaiming: "How sweet and cool you have made it in here, Mary! I declare it is pleasant to come home."

"I'm very glad you think so, dear," was the pleased reply.

"It seems more pleasant than ever to me to-day, after what I've seen."

"Why, where have you been?"

"I went to see those poor children I was telling you about the other day—and what do you think? Their mother died suddenly the night before last. They are wretchedly poor. I never was so shocked in my life."

"Poor, poor children!" said Mary, pityingly.

"And that's not all," continued her sister. "Their father went off and left them as soon as he found out about the mother."

"Oh, Helen, how sad! Can't we do something for them?"

"That's just what I've been puzzling my brain to find out," was the answer.

"Who will bury the poor woman?"

"The town, of course. They have no friends—at least, nobody seems to know anything about them."

"Poor things!" again said Mary.

"I'm going to help you sew some now, Mary." And Helen slipped on her thimble, threaded a needle, and began to stitch away industriously.

For some minutes the sisters worked on in silence, then Mary looked up and said, softly, her sweet smile lighting up the wan face: "'And the King shall answer and say unto them : Verily I say unto you, inasmuch as ye have done it unto one of the least of these my brethren, ye have done it unto me.' Sister, we must help those children."

"That's easily said, Mary dear, but how are we to do it? Oh, here comes Dr. Barrett! Now suppose we ask him about the boy? Maybe he can do something for him. We'll do it!" And the young girl arose and went to the door to welcome the genial-faced old gentleman, who had alighted from his buggy and was now coming up the walk.

Dr. Barrett was an old friend of the sisters. He had been the family physician ever since the girls could remember. He had always been their friend, and since the death of their parents seemed more like a father to them. He had attended Mary from her first illness, and insisted on coming every once in a while to see her, even when she was in her usual health. She was never really well. The girls were always glad to see his buggy stop before their gate.

"Well, how are we to-day?" was his cheery greeting, as he put his head in at the door.

"No; I can't come in. I've a new horse, and he won't stand long—Whoa, there, Ned! Can't you wait a minute?" he called to the restless animal, which, finding itself free, was not slow to take advantage of his liberty, perhaps thinking it a good time to go for a stroll on his own account. He was interrupted, however, in time to prevent any such undesirable proceeding.

"I must get a boy. That horse won't stand unless he has some one to hold him," panted the doctor, as he again ascended the steps, having given Mr. Ned in charge of a small lad.

"A boy, did you say, Dr. Barrett?" cried Helen while Mary listened attentively.

"Yes, 'a boy.' Is there anything wonderful about that?" returned the doctor.

"Well, yes," retorted Helen, mischievously. "There is something wonderful about it."

"Indeed? I'd like to know what it is, then."

"There's something both wonderful and fortunate about your wanting a boy just now. We have one all ready for you, and you *must* take him, you know."

"Is there a 'must' about it too?"

"Yes, indeed; and a penalty to pay if you disobey."

"What will the penalty be, pray?"

"Why, we shan't like you any more."

"Speak for yourself, Helen," put in Mary, laughing.

"Now you keep out of this, Mary, and let me manage things," said Helen, playfully shaking her finger at her sister. Then turning again to the doctor, she asked, with mock gravity: "Do you accept the conditions, sir?"

"I do," answered he, in the same tone.

"So you promise to take the boy we have for you?"

"I promise, most solemnly, to take the boy, if he suits me; and not to, if he doesn't."

"Now you are too bad, Dr. Barrett," cried Helen. "But I shall send him to your office, just the same."

"All right; send him up," was the reply. Then, dropping his

jesting tone, he said: "I guess he'll do. If you are so anxious about the matter, I'll try him for a while."

"Oh, I'm pretty sure he will suit you. He seems to be such a steady, independent sort of boy." And then she told the old gentleman the story we already know, to which he listened with interest, expressing sympathy and promising to do what he could for Clarence, if he proved worthy.

After a pleasant little chat, the good doctor arose to go, telling Helen to "be sure and send the boy up as soon as possible." This she was more than willing to promise.

"I consider that a special providence, Mary," she said, when they were once more alone. "To think that Dr. Barrett should want a boy at this time!"

"'He shall give thee the desires of thine heart,'" repeated her sister, reverently.

Helen smiled. "It seems to me that you have a text for everything. But now it's about time for tea." And she began putting away her sewing.

It was true, as her sister had said. Mary had a verse, or part of a verse, to fit in almost everywhere. The invalid loved her Bible. It was her constant companion, and she knew it well.

CHAPTER IV
Provided For

Clarence was quite as determined that he would not wear Tom Greene's clothes to his mother's funeral as he had been that he would not go to Tom Greene's home the day before; so, leaving his sister and Mrs. Greene together, he climbed up to his attic, and having succeeded in finding materials, proceeded to draw together, as best he could, the rents in the garments his poor mother had been attempting to mend on the last sad day of her life. The articles consisted of a jacket and trousers; and he was working away industriously, if not skillfully, when Corinne, who had missed him, stole quietly upon him.

"Whatever are you doing, Clarence?" she asked.

"Oh, nothing much," he answered; "only fixing these things to put on."

"But you won't need them, Clarence. Mrs. Greene has brought a nice suit of her Tom's for you to wear. Why, you know that!"

"Yes, I know it well enough. I shan't wear it, though."

"Not wear the clothes Mrs. Greene brought!"

"No; I'd rather wear the worst kind of rags than put on Tom Greene's things and have him throw it in my face afterward."

"Oh, but, Clarence, Mrs. Greene will be angry! And she has been so good to us! I am to wear a dress of Lizzie's."

"Oh, it's all right about you; they wouldn't bother you. Just let me do as I want to about this, Corrie, there's a good girl. I'll make it all right with Mrs. Greene. She needn't know why I don't want to wear the clothes she brought. Run away down, now, won't you?"

Corrie did as she was told; and her brother, finishing his

mending, put on the garments and went down.

"Why, Clarence, I thought you were putting on the suit I brought for you. Hurry, now, and get it on," cried Mrs. Greene.

"I'd rather wear these things, Mrs. Greene, please," stammered the boy.

"Why, what on earth—" began the puzzled woman impatiently. But she was interrupted by a knock on the door.

There was no further time to spend in talking, for the hearse was waiting for its burden. The mother, in her rough coffin was placed within, and the two children followed it to the burial place, where a short service was read; and then the earth was thrown in upon all that was mortal that remained of their parent. The two children had cried so much that they could do nothing now but stand and look on in a dazed sort of way. When all was over they turned sadly and walked away.

Mrs. Greene was waiting for them at the door of the little cottage. She had determined not to notice any further the boy's refusal to wear the clothes. She told the children that she was waiting to take them home with her to pass the night. To her astonishment, Clarence said, quietly:

"You have been very kind to us, Mrs. Greene, and we're very thankful to you for all you have done for us; but if you please, ma'am, I am going to stay here tonight. Corrie can do as she likes; she can go if she wants to."

"No, no, Clarence; I'll stay with you," whispered his sister, although the vision of Mrs. Greene's cozy, neat rooms was a great deal more inviting than the dingy, dreary cottage. But she was unwilling to leave her brother alone. He was all she had to look up to, and she wanted to be near him.

"Well, Clarence Burton," said Mrs. Greene, when she had recovered enough to say anything, "I didn't think you were such an ungrateful, headstrong boy. But there; that's all one has a right to expect from such people." And she walked away with an angry air.

"Oh, Clarence! I thought she would be angry," said Corinne, regretfully.

"Well, I can't help it," answered her brother. "Of course, I'm thankful for what she has done; but that doesn't make me want to go to her house. I couldn't go there, and that's all about it." He turned and entered the house, and Corinne followed.

The night seemed very long and dreary, especially to the little girl, who was a timid, nervous child; and day-light was a welcome sight. Good Mrs. Greene, although she was angry at the boy's persistent refusal to come to her home, could not bring herself to forget the forlorn children entirely; so she sent Lizzie over with some breakfast, which they were glad to receive, and for which they thanked her warmly.

Early that morning their friend, Miss Gray, came to deliver her message to Clarence, who received it with real pleasure. Having done this, she was about to tell Corinne to get ready to go home with her for the day, when Miss Rachel Penrose unceremoniously entered.

As I have already said, Miss Rachel was the owner of the wretched old cottage; and she had come to tell the children that it would be no longer their home. When she heard that the boy had been offered a situation, she nodded her head approvingly, and said that, "seein' as the boy's provided for, I guess I'll take the girl. She's likely to be of service to run errands and wash dishes and such."

And so it was settled, and the cottage was closed. Corinne went to her new home with Miss Rachel, and Clarence went with Miss Gray, who was to show him the way to Dr. Barrett's office. He found that good gentleman just getting ready to go out.

"Oh so you're 'the boy' are you?" he said, adjusting his gold-rimmed spectacles to get a better view of him.

"What is your name?"

"Clarence Burton, sir."

"Clarence, is it, eh? Well, that's a good name. Now, Clarence, I've got to go out for a while. Just turn about in here, and rub things up generally; for everything is at sixes and sevens, as the saying goes. I had a good smart boy, but he was taken sick and compelled to go home, and I haven't been able to find another to suit me, until I heard about you."

Clarence, much pleased at his hearty reception, promised to do his best to please the good doctor.

After giving directions as to how he wanted things "rubbed up," and charging him to be careful, he went out, leaving the boy feeling very strange and queer. He set to work, however—clumsily enough, to be sure, at first, but with the determination to do his best to give satisfaction.

Meanwhile, Corinne had gone with Miss Penrose. "Miss Rachel Penrose, Seamstress," was the announcement the plate on her door made to the passers-by. Miss Rachel was a spinster who supported herself by her needle. Not that she was wholly dependent upon it for a living; for besides owning the house in which she lived and the cottage in which the Burtons had lived, she had a snug sum of money in the savings bank. As she was a good seamstress, she had a large run of custom and was well paid for her work.

But Miss Rachel was stingy. "Saving" was her besetting sin. Now the habit of saving, when exercised wisely and properly, is a virtue; but when saving means depriving one's self, and others, of the actual necessities of life, in order to lay away money for the sake of simply possessing, then it becomes a vice.

It had become so with Miss Rachel. Every cent she spent was parted with as though it were a drop of blood, without which she could not possibly survive. She counted her coals, she counted the potatoes, she meted out everything with the smallest measurement possible. A bright fire, in her opinion, was a waste, and enough to eat entirely unnecessary.

Such was the woman with whom our little friend Corinne had found a home. The child had led an idle, useless life. Her mother had made no effort whatever to train her in any way. Indeed, she had paid but little attention to her children since their earliest years. She had given way altogether to despondency, and had lost all energy and ambition, doing hardly anything, save to sit and brood bitterly and rebelliously over the fate that had shut out from her the light of happiness. Had Mrs. Burton been a Christian she would not have done so, but would have sought to rear her boy and girl properly, and would have striven to accept her lot at least cheerfully. But she was not a Christian, and, therefore, lived as one without hope. She had been born and reared in the country, but had been early deprived of her parents. She had been cared for by strangers, and had grown to be a giddy, thoughtless girl. She had met and formed the acquaintance of James Burton; and although she well knew that he was given to hard drinking, she married him. There had been friendly people who had advised her to do otherwise, and had warned her of the dangers before her; but she was headstrong, and so chose her own way and found it full of thorns. She had thought she knew best, and cherished many bright hopes for a happy future. But alas! like the man in the Lord's sermon, she had built upon the sand. And the rain descended, and the floods came, and the winds blew, and beat upon her house; and it fell, and great was the fall of it.

When she could, she would not hear; and when she saw her bright prospects slipping from her she had nothing to cling to—no hope in this world nor in the world to come. Was it any wonder, then, that she had drifted into the wretched creature she became? With their two little children, the unhappy couple left their country home and came to N— — — to live in the old cottage, which was only fit to be torn down. For this they paid but little, but more than the place was worth; its owner saw to that. Proud and mortified, Mrs. Burton had shut herself up, alone with her wretchedness, and had repelled all attempts on the part of her neighbors to befriend her. To pay the bit of house rent was now pretty much the extent of James Burton's provision for his family; and so it was but a short while before the abused and despondent wife lost all care as to whether things were kept in order or not. The children went to school as long as their clothes lasted; and, be it said to her credit, their mother did mend and fix over their scanty wardrobe as long as it could be done, and some of the hottest battles between the wretched pair were fought that she might obtain decent clothing for them. But she wearied of the struggle at last, and the garments had become so worn that they were no longer fit to wear to school, especially as the more favored but cruelly thoughtless children had taken advantage of this to nickname the brother and sister "ragamuffins"; and so they went to school no more. Clarence did odd jobs whenever he could get them to do, and but for this the lot of his mother and Corinne would have been even harder than it was.

These were the surroundings amid which Corinne Burton had passed her young life. It is but natural to conclude that it was a sudden change from such a home as I have already described to one where everything was as prim and orderly as its prim mistress.

Miss Rachel Penrose had had a girl to do her housework, but she had been taken ill, and had gone to her home just previous to the death of Mrs. Burton. It was on the day when Miss Rachel had gone to the cottage at the request of Mrs. Greene, that she conceived the idea of supplying the place of her former maid-of-all-work with the homeless little Corinne, persuading herself into the belief that she was very benevolent and charitable to take a motherless child and provide her with a home and food, which she would pay for by the help she would render in her home.

CHAPTER V

Corinne's New Home

A month had elapsed since Corinne first entered her new home. It was now July. One warm morning, Miss Rachel, seated in her accustomed place, sewing, was dividing her attention between her work and the little girl, who was washing and polishing the front windows. She had rubbed the panes again and again, until her arms ached, and still Miss Rachel declared that they were not fit to look at; "but you can't stand there rubbing all day, so they'll have to do, I 'spose. Go, now, and scrub that kitchen floor, and mind, if it don't suit me when you're done, I'll make you do it over till it does; and don't be long about it, either."

The small tired arms and hands hastened to get pail and brush, and to scrub, scrub, scrub, only to be told that the floor looked "as bad as before." Poor child! it had been this way ever since the day she came there from the cottage, and it seemed to her that, hard as her lot had been before, it was doubly so now. Nothing but hard work from morning until night. Not a moment of the day which she could call her own, her hard task mistress begrudging her the time spent in eating the meagre food she allowed her; and sometimes even the privilege of eating at all was on the slightest pretext denied her. As a general thing, the child arose from her bed hungry, and retired to it again hungry when the day was over. She cried herself to sleep nearly every night, partly from weariness, partly from grief.

If Miss Rachel had only spoken a kind word to her once in a while, she thought she would not have minded so much about the rest; but the hard features of the seamstress had no smiles for the sad-faced little Corinne, and the thin lips voiced no words for her, more pleasant than an order to do something, or a complaint that some other thing had not been satisfactorily done. It was no wonder, then, that the child grew thinner than ever, as the weary days dragged themselves by.

Clarence had been to see her once one day, while Miss Rachel was out. The doctor could not spare him often, he said. He looked well and happy, and Corinne had been so glad to see him that she had disliked to mar the pleasure of his visit with complaints. Young as she was, she felt that nothing could be done about the matter, so she had given herself up to the enjoyment of the moment.

This visit had cheered the little girl very much, and her heart felt lighter that night as she lay down to rest, and she thought of her brother a long time before she fell asleep. He had talked to her about his situation and the kindness of his employer, and had confided to her his plans, which seemed to her simple mind nothing short of wonderful; and the thought of these plans made her forget, for the time being, that for her the old, dreary, uneventful life would commence again with the morning light.

Clarence had drawn the conclusion, from the very tidy appearance of the house, that his sister was fortunate in having such a home, especially since Corinne had made no complaints, and had evaded his question as to whether she liked to live there.

The boy himself was doing well. Naturally quick, and scrupulously honest and truthful, he had proved very useful to the good doctor. He felt that he had now "the chance," as he expressed it, for which he had wished so long; and he had fully made up his mind to improve it to the utmost.

The doctor, seeing that the boy was ambitious to make something of himself, sympathized with him and gave him some old school books, which he found stowed away in a corner of his bookcase. These books the boy studied carefully during his leisure moments, with occasionally a little help from the doctor. He had told Corinne that he meant to make a man of himself, and also that his fixed determination was to make a home for her; and when he had pictured to her that home, and the many comforts it was to contain, she had been too happy to do anything but clasp her hands and say,

"Oh, Clarence!"

These were the plans that brightened the hours of the night after her brother's visit. Indeed, the memory of that visit and the vision of the home her brother was to make for them was the subject of her thoughts for days afterward.

She did not know it, but there was another glimmer of light coming into her dull life. It came after this fashion: Her friend, Miss Gray, had been absent during the summer holidays with her sister. They had been to pay a visit to one of their father's relatives who lived in the country, several hours' ride from N— — —.

It was the latter part of August when they returned.

One of the first things Helen Gray did was to call on Miss Rachel Penrose, ostensibly to have a chat, but in reality to see how Corinne was getting along. The child was out at the time, so she seated herself and began talking to Miss Rachel, who, having always on hand an abundance of topics upon which to talk, was by no means averse to having a little conversation. In answer to her queries, she told her caller all that had happened during her absence; not that there had been any very important happenings, but such as there had been were made the most of.

Her visitor listened apparently much interested, but inwardly wishing that Corinne would come. At length, just as she was about to go, the child came in, looking hot and tired, and so thin and wretched that Helen could scarcely repress an exclamation of pity. But feeling that the keen gray eyes of the seamstress were looking at her sharply, and fearing that she might make trouble for the little girl, she checked herself, and simply said: "Why, Corinne, how do you do?"

Corinne, overjoyed at sight of the kind familiar face, had noticed the fleeting expression of sympathy in it. She was a little disappointed at the indifferent tone of Miss Gray's voice when she spoke to her. She tried, however, to smile and answer cheerfully, as she knew Miss Rachel desired her to do; but it was a very pitiful smile, and she was only too glad to hurry away before her stern guardian should notice the quivering lip and gathering teardrops.

Helen had seen enough to convince her that the poor motherless child was unhappy and oppressed. She soon rose to go, saying as she did so, as carelessly as she could: "Miss Rachel, I would like it if you would let Corinne come to see me next Sunday afternoon. Does she go to Sunday-school?"

"No," was the answer, "she's no time to go; besides, what would the likes of her want there? It would just put notions in her head, and she'd be getting above her place."

"But —," gently remonstrated Miss Gray, startled out of her caution. "But you are a church member yourself, and surely you would not want the child grow up like a heathen?"

"I'd wish you to know, miss, that I know what's my duty, and what's not, too," retorted Miss Rachel; adding "and I need none of your telling."

"I beg your pardon, Miss Penrose," Helen hastened to say, feeling that she had injured her own cause. "I beg your pardon! Of course, you know your duty; I did not mean to say you did not; but won't you let Corinne come to see my sister some Sunday afternoons? She would like so much to have her to teach. You know she is an invalid, and can't go out much, and she does long so to have a class in the Sunday-school. It would please her to have Corinne. You will let her come, won't you?"

"Well," said Miss Rachel, slowly, somewhat mollified by the coaxing tones, "well, I can't promise for often, but maybe she can come sometimes, seeing it's you as wants her."

"Thank you," said Helen, congratulating herself upon gaining her point so easily. "May she come next Sunday?"

"I'll see about it; maybe so" was the reply. And the visitor took her leave.

When Helen reached home, she found her sister lying upon the sofa, with her eyes closed. Thinking her asleep, she stole softly to her side, and stood looking down into the face so sadly pinched and drawn by sickness and pain, the face so dear to her; and the thought that it looked thinner than ever caused her heart to beat, with the dread that one day she might miss from her side the only being left upon earth whom she could claim as her own. But only for an instant did she allow this thought to tarry; stooping, she lightly kissed the brow of the supposed sleeper. As she did so, the dark eyes unclosed, and Mary looked up into her face with her sweet smile, and said: "Did you think I was asleep? "

"Why, of course I did, you naughty child," returned her sister, pretending to be displeased. "What do you mean by shamming in that way?"

"I wasn't shamming—at least, I didn't mean to be."

"What were you doing then? You said you were not asleep," said Helen, curiously.

"I was just thinking, as I do lots of times when I am all alone."

"Thinking of what, dear?"

"Oh, of different things. Just then I was wondering if I had a mission, and what it was."

"Well, that's easily enough answered," said Helen. "Your mission is to be my sweet little sister and companion; isn't that mission enough for you?"

"No, Helen, I don't think it is; it's almost too pleasant to be considered so; besides, if there's any mission about it, it belongs to you. There is little I can do for you, and you do all for me. I am not necessary to you, but you are to me."

"Now, there's just where you are wrong, my dear; you are altogether and entirely necessary to me. But if it will please you better, my mission is to care for you, and yours to care for me; will that do?"

"Yes, that will do very well, so far as it goes."

"'So far as it goes'; you ungrateful girl! What do you mean?"

"Why, I mean that I'd like to do something for some one else besides you. I want to feel that I am doing good to somebody."

"Oh, if that's all, I think your wish can be gratified."

Helen had left her sister's side during this conversation, and had busied herself with laying the table for the evening meal. Having set the tea to draw, she came and sat down near Mary's sofa, and taking some sewing from the little workstand beside her, began to stitch away.

"How can my wish be gratified?" asked the invalid, watching the deft fingers of her sister with her large liquid eyes.

"Just this way," was the reply: "That poor child, Corinne Burton—you remember Corinne, don't you, whose mother died just a little while before we went to the country?"

"Oh, yes," answered Mary. "And whose father went off and left her and her brother all alone. I remember Corinne. What about her?"

"Well, she went to live with that prim Miss Rachel Penrose, the seamstress. I was so glad, because being apparently a very exemplary woman, I was quite sure she would have a good home."

"Well, didn't she?" queried Mary, anxiously.

"The home is good enough," said Helen, "but she isn't treated well."

"How do you know?"

"Because I went to see her to-day, and she looks very thin and weak; as if she were overworked. Miss Penrose spoke so crossly to her too; in fact, the child looks more miserable than she did when she was living at home in that wretched old shanty."

"Oh, Helen!" exclaimed Mary. "How sorry I am for her! But what can you do, and what has she to do with what we were talking about just now?"

"A great deal. I've coaxed Miss Penrose to let her come here Sunday afternoons—partly that Corinne may have a pleasant change, and partly because I thought you would like to give her some Bible lessons."

"Yes, indeed, Helen dear; that's just what I should like of all things."

"I thought you would; and you can do the poor child ever so much good. But come, Mary, you must have your tea." And rising, she placed her arm about her sister's waist and tenderly led her to her seat at the table.

CHAPTER VI

A Disappointment

Corinne awoke on the Sunday morning following Miss Gray's visit with a new and strange sensation. This was the day she was to go, for the first time, to the home of the kind young lady whose smiling face was seldom out of her mind now. With a light heart she arose, and began her usual tasks with unusual cheerfulness, which did not fail to make itself apparent to Miss Rachel, who of course guessed what it meant.

Miss Rachel was pharisaical in her make-up, and always made a great show of piety. Especially did she do so on Sundays. She invariably attended church in the morning, rain or shine, snow or blow. She considered when she had done this that her duty was done, so far as church was concerned. That Corinne should go sometimes never suggested itself to her as at all necessary. She was careful to leave sufficient work to last the child until she came home, and woe to her if it was not done. In the afternoon, after everything was cleared up, she made the child, who had just begun to read a little, take the Bible and read aloud a chapter. Not one that contained anything she could understand, but such as the twenty-eighth or twenty-ninth of Numbers, all about sacrifices, etc. The majority of the words Corinne was obliged to spell, and altogether it was very dull, dry, hard work, and made her eyes and head ache. As she was never allowed to have the Bible any other day except Sunday, she knew nothing of its contents save the part which was given her to read on that day. Miss Rachel considered that she was acting the part of a Christian guardian in making the child plod though such verses as: "And one goat, for a sin-offering; beside the continual burnt-offering; and his meat-offering, and his drink-offering." What it all meant Corinne had not the slightest idea, and indeed I am not at all sure that Miss Rachel knew much more about it than did she. The beautiful stories of "Joseph," "Daniel," "Samuel," and others were unknown to the little girl, and the precious truths of the New Testament—the history of the birth, life, and death of the dear Saviour—were all hidden treasures of which she was entirely ignorant.

In one respect, however, Sundays were a relief from week days, and that was that she was sent to bed immediately after tea. But it was all very dull and lonely, for she was never allowed to go out except on errands.

Was it strange then, that the prospect of a change of any kind should delight her? Willingly and swiftly did Corinne perform her tasks while Miss Rachel was at church, taking especial care to do them just as well as she could. The dinner, which differed but little from the week-day meal, was all ready and on the table when she came home. When it was over, and the dishes cleared away, as Miss Rachel had said nothing about it, she ventured to ask if she might "go to Miss Gray's now." She had had no thought but that the partial promise would be fulfilled, but to her dismay Miss Rachel told her coldly that she could not go, as she was going out herself, and she did not wish to leave the house left with no one in it.

Corinne was bitterly disappointed. She turned quickly away to hide the hot tears that forced themselves from her eyes, and which she dared not let fall in her guardian's presence. They fell thick and fast, however, when the front door closed upon her. Corinne cried for a while as if her heart would break, and the tears were still falling when she was startled by a rap on the door. Thinking it was Miss Rachel who had changed her mind about going out, and had returned, she hurriedly dried her eyes before opening the door. To her surprise and delight, she found that it was her brother.

"Oh, Clarence!" she cried.

"Hello, Corrie!" returned he.

"I'm so glad you've come."

"So am I. But what's the matter? You've been crying. Has anybody hurt you? "

"No," answered Corinne, hesitatingly. She disliked to worry her brother with her troubles when she knew he could do her no good.

"Well, what were you crying about?" persisted Clarence, with an air that said plainly, "I mean to know, so you might as well hurry up and tell."

So Corinne told him the story of her disappointment. "The mean old thing!" exclaimed Clarence, angrily.

"Never mind about it now, Clarence. It's all right since you're here. I'd have missed seeing you if I had gone."

"But it *was* mean in her, and I'd like to tell her so," still fumed the boy.

"Oh, well, that wouldn't do any good, and would make her all the harder on me. Come, now, don't let's talk any more about that. Tell me something about yourself." And she seated herself beside him.

"Well, Corrie," began Clarence, twisting about uncomfortably, "here's another rub. I most hate to tell you."

"What is it? Tell me. I guess I'll not mind."

"Well, I hope you won't; but I going to L— — — next week," said the boy, abruptly, hurrying to get the unpleasant task over.

"Going to L— — — next week?" repeated Corinne, as if she did not know what the words meant. "Oh, Clarence! going to leave me?" she cried, as she began to realize their meaning.

"Now, see here, Corrie," her brother hastened to say, consolingly, "I'm going away to earn money to make that home we were talking about when I was here last time." And Clarence gently patted his sister's head, which she had laid on his shoulder.

"Why, ain't you making money where you are?" sobbed Corinne.

"Oh, I don't get much besides my clothes and board at the doctor's. He's kind to me, to be sure, and gives me a little extra change once in a while. I've been saving up, and I've got a little more than enough to take me to L— — —, where I am sure I can get a place in a store of some kind. I'd like that kind of work ever so much better; and then, you know, I'm sure to make more money," he said, emphasizing the argument which he thought most likely to recommend itself to his sister.

"I'm awful sorry that you've got such a hard one to live with," he continued, "but don't you mind; it'll all come out right one of these days. I'll go by Miss Gray's as I go home, and tell her all about it. Maybe she can get Miss Rachel to let you come next Sunday."

"Yes, do, Clarence," said Corinne, drying her eyes, and feeling a little comforted as she listened while Clarence drew bright pictures of what was to be in the future.

When her brother rose to go, she could not help the tears coming again, as she thought how soon he was to leave her.

"Don't fret so, Corrie," said he. "It's the best thing I can do, and you'll believe so when you hear that I've a good place and am saving money, for I mean to save every cent I can. It won't be long, so don't take on so about my going. I'll write to you as soon as I get something to do, and then I'll write often afterward, and you'll know just how I'm getting along. That'll be nice, won't it, Corrie?"

"Yes," answered the little girl, smiling faintly through her tears. "Can you write a letter, Clarence?" she asked, admiringly.

"Oh, of course, I can't write so very well, but I can write some — you know I could before I left school, and I've been practicing a good bit lately. Dr. Barrett has helped me some too, when he wasn't busy. He's heard me read and spell. I mean to go to night school when I get settled. Now, good-bye, Corrie; I must go. I'll come in again before I go." And with another "good-bye," Clarence was gone.

It was not so very long after he left, that another tap at the door announced the fact that Miss Rachel had returned. Poor Corinne had entirely forgotten, so busy had she been with her brother, that she should have been getting tea ready; and now, as Miss Rachel glanced in surprise around the room, she remembered it for the first time.

"Well, miss, what have you been doing ever since I've been gone not to have tea ready?"

Corinne stammered that Clarence had been there, and she had been talking to him but had forgotten it was nearly tea time.

"Very well," was the sharp response; "that shows that *you* don't stand in need of your supper very badly, so you can go to bed. I'll get my own."

Poor Corinne went silently up stairs to her bare little room, and throwing herself upon the bed sobbed violently. She thought that surely there could not live a more unhappy little girl than herself. After she had cried until it seemed as if she could cry no more, she sat up on the bed, dried her swollen eyes, and looked listlessly about the room.

There was nothing in it but her bed and an old broken stand. Indeed, it was too small to hold anything else. There was an old empty closet in one corner, the door of which had been missing for many years. Upon a shelf at the top the wandering eyes of Corinne spied something small and brown. It looked like a book, and the child, being lonely, and glad of anything for a change, determined to get it, if for nothing else than to divert her attention from the hunger that was making her feel almost sick.

She pulled the old stand across the floor as carefully and noiselessly as she could for fear of attracting the attention of the occupant of the room below. Mounting the rickety thing, she reached up and took down the old book and wiped the thick coating of dust from its dingy cover. Clambering down from the stand, and replacing it, she seated herself again on the side of the bed and opened the antiquated volume. It was still daylight, so that she could see that the book was a Bible. At first she was disappointed, the sight of the yellow pages bringing vividly to her mind the Sunday afternoon readings. But she was so lonely that even these would help pass away some of the time, so she went as near the window as she could get. It was too high up for her to reach its sill without the aid of the old stand, which she was afraid to attempt to move again. So she stood beneath the window, in order to see clearly, and opened the book again. This time she opened it at the New Testament. Glancing down the page for something that looked as if she could understand it, her eye caught the words: "Casting all your care upon him; for he careth for you."

Again and again, she slowly and carefully spelt it out until the words were fixed in her mind. What comforting words they were! She did not understand much about them, for, poor child! she had had no one to teach her, but they sounded so good that long after it grew too dark for her to see more, she had kept repeating them.

At last, with a sigh, she arose, and placing the Bible still open at the precious verse, under her pillow, she went to bed and was soon fast asleep.

CHAPTER VII

Corinne's Visit

Clarence, mindful of his promise to Corinne, stopped on his way home, to explain to Miss Gray why she had not come that afternoon.

The sisters were sorry, particularly on the little girl's account; for they knew that she must have been very much disappointed at not being allowed to come.

They were sorry too to hear that Clarence was going to leave N———. Still they agreed with him, when he told them of his hopes and aspirations, that it would be best. They promised him that they would see after his sister, and assured him that she should be placed in another home as soon as one could be procured, and Miss Rachel could be induced to give her up.

Helen secretly anticipated trouble in getting the consent of the exacting woman to any such proceeding; for she well knew that Corinne was the means of saving her self-constituted guardian no small sum, since she paid her no wages. The scanty food and poor clothing the child received was but little reward for the quantity of labor required of her.

But Helen said nothing of her thoughts to the others; for she knew that they would worry the poor boy, who was so bent on making a way in the world for himself and his beloved sister. His heart was much lighter when he resumed his walk homeward; and many were the castles in the air he built as he walked.

Helen and Mary Gray sat and talked long after he had gone, but could arrive at no solution of the perplexing problem as to how and where a home was to be found for their little protégé. They would have taken her into their own; but the salary Helen received for her teaching was barely sufficient to provide for the wants of herself and her sister; and she well knew that it could not be made to cover the cost of feeding and clothing another.

"Well," said Mary, laughing softly, "we've talked and talked, and suggested and suggested, and we're not a bit wiser now than when we began. Don't you think it would be a good idea to lay the whole matter before One who is wiser than we, and leave the result to him?"

"Why, dear, it's just the thing we ought to do," replied her sister. "What short-sighted people we are, to be sure! We sit, and worry, and fret, and plan, all to no purpose; entirely forgetful of him who 'speaks, and none can hinder.' Yes, we *will* leave it to him, Mary."

And so, from two devout hearts went up, that night, two earnest petitions in behalf of the poor little waif who was even then unconsciously learning to cast her cares upon One who was able to help her bear them.

Clarence went to see his sister once more before he left N— — —, but only saw her long enough to say "Good-bye," and whisper a word or two of assurance that it would not be very many years before they would meet again, to spend the rest of their lives together. "Of course, I shall try and come to see you when I can; but I don't want to lose any time. I shall be sure to write, though; and if you can't manage to make out my writing, Miss Helen will read it for you, I know. Good-bye, Corrie."

"Good-bye, Clarence."

With this he was gone. It was really a good thing for the child that Miss Rachel kept her so busy that day that she had no time to cry until she went to bed; and then she was so tired that she fell asleep before she had cried half as much as she had intended to.

The next day it was the same, and the next, and the next; until at last she gave up trying to find time to cry over her brother's departure. And so the tedious days dragged wearily along.

Miss Rachel's conscience was not so callous but that the sight of the child's patient, uncomplaining ways made a little impression upon it; and so, a month after Clarence had gone, one Sunday afternoon, when the house had been put in order after the dinner, Miss Rachel surprised

Corinne by telling her that she might "go up to that Miss Gray's awhile before tea," bidding her be sure and "be back in time to get it ready."

Corinne was surprised, because Miss Rachel had steadily refused before to allow her to go.

The little girl walked through the streets to her friend's house in a way quite different from that in which she had fancied she would go, and from the way in which she would have gone before Clarence went away. She felt so sad and lonely, that even the prospect of an afternoon with her beloved Miss Gray failed to cheer her.

She found the sisters sitting in their pleasant little sitting room. There was a small fire crackling in the open grate; for the autumn was advancing, and the invalid found the afternoons chilly.

Helen had been reading aloud, but had paused to make some comment on what she had just read, when the click of the gate latch caused her to look up inquiringly.

"Why, it's Corinne," she cried, as she opened the door in answer to the timid knock.

"Come right in, my dear. I'm glad to see you. I was thinking about you this very day."

"And so was I," chimed in Mary, holding out her wasted hand to Corinne.

"Helen," added she, mysteriously, "maybe it's coming."

"Maybe what is coming, dear?"

"Why, what we were talking about that Sunday night." Helen laughed, a little amused laugh; but more was coming than she had any idea of.

They made Corinne feel at home, and seated her in a low chair, to rest herself, for she seemed tired.

Helen was more shocked than ever, to see how thin and weak the child looked. She could scarcely restrain her tears at sight of the pitiful, pinched features, and large, sunken eyes.

Seeing that Corinne was rather shy of her sister, whom she had not seen before, Helen put on her hat, and saying that she was going out for a walk, while Mary had Corinne to keep her company, left the two together to get acquainted. This they were not long in doing, for Mary knew just how to put the timid little creature at ease; and in a wonderfully short time they were chatting away about Clarence and his hopes and prospects, as freely as if they had known each other all their lives. Presently Mary asked Corinne if she would not like to have her read some in the Bible.

"Oh, yes, indeed" said the child, eagerly. "I should like it so much." And then she told the story of the Bible she had found on the shelf in the old closet, on that memorable Sunday afternoon.

She told her about the verse she had first noticed, and how she had, ever since, tried to get up a little earlier than usual, in order to read some in the precious book. She had found out what the words meant now; for she had read the story again and again, and already loved the dear Saviour who had died for her, and really cared for her. And once, when she took the big Bible that was down stairs to read the usual Sunday afternoon chapter, she had asked Miss Rachel if she might read one of her favorite chapters instead. But that good woman had told her to read what she was told to read, and she would be doing what she ought to do. So she had plodded on, comforting herself with the thought that she could read her "own dear Bible," as she styled it, "in the morning."

It was a great relief to tell this to the gentle Mary, who listened sympathizingly, and who read again to her some comforting words from the good book. And then she talked to her so sweetly, and explained everything so clearly.

"Do you love the dear Lord about whom we have been reading, Corinne?" she asked, softly, closing the Bible.

"Yes, I do, Miss Mary," answered the child, reverently. "I loved him as soon as I read about him in the good book. And ever since I read that beautiful verse about casting all our cares on him, I've tried to cast mine on him. For sometimes I feel so weak and sick that I think I will just fall down; and I ask him to take some of my cares, and help me to bear them."

"Repeat that verse, Corinne," said Mary. "I love it too."

"'Casting all your care upon him; for he careth for you,'" repeated the child.

Helen had entered the room while she was doing so, but Corinne did not notice her. She just kept on repeating the verse over and over again, as if she did not know what she was doing. The last time the words were only whispered; and, to Mary's alarm, the little girl's head dropped on her bosom, and she would have fallen to the floor, had not Helen caught her.

"Oh, Helen, what is the matter with her?"

"She has fainted. I guess she will be all right by-and-by. The poor little thing is overworked and underfed. I declare it's a shame."

They applied such remedies as suggested themselves, and at length Corinne regained consciousness, but she was so weak, and looked so ill, that Helen said she should not leave them that night. She quickly undressed the little girl, and made her comfortable in bed, telling her that she meant her to stay there until she was better, and that she was going to tell Miss Rachel why she did not come home.

Corinne soon dropped off into a heavy sleep; and Helen, promising to "be back in next to no time," hurried out on her errand. "Of course," she thought, "the child is only tired out. She will be better in the morning."

She found Miss Penrose in a very unpleasant mood, because of Corinne's long absence; but the woman was quite "taken aback," to use her own expression, when she heard how matters stood, especially since her conscience told her that Corinne's illness could be traced to her door. She made no objection, when Helen Gray told her that the child should stay with her until she was quite well. Indeed, she seemed really pleased at the arrangement, as it would relieve her.

CHAPTER VIII
Corinne's Illness

When morning came it found our little friend in a high fever, and moaning and groaning as if in great pain.

Helen, now thoroughly alarmed, hastened to call in Dr. Barrett. When he saw the child he shook his head gravely.

"She is in for a long and severe spell, my dear. Who is she?"

"Why, she's Clarence Burton's little sister."

"Well, she had better be sent to the hospital," said the doctor, looking up from the prescription he was writing.

"No, indeed; we wouldn't think of such a thing," cried Helen, indignantly.

"Well, well; it's all right—just as you like; and anyway, I hardly think it would be safe to move her now. I'll be in to see her again this afternoon." And the good old doctor hurried away.

Instead of growing better, Corinne grew worse, and when the doctor came in the afternoon he said that her illness would go hard with her, for she was so very weak.

"You don't think she will die; do you, doctor?" inquired Helen; and Mary listened anxiously for his reply. This little patient, motherless creature had, all unwittingly, appealed strongly to their sympathies.

"I can't say whether she will die or not; that is with one wiser than I. I do know that she is very ill; but young people can stand a good deal of sickness and come out all right in the end. We'll do all we can for her, and hope for the best."

Having given directions as to what was to be done. Dr. Barrett turned to go. Pausing with his hand on the door knob, he said:

"You needn't bother about the bill, girls. I shall come as often as I think best and do as I please about the pay, you know. If you can take the responsibility of nursing this child, I guess I can afford to do the prescribing. Oh, you needn't thank me," he added, as the sisters looked at him in grateful astonishment; "I only mean that you two sha'n't have all the credit of being good." And away went the kind-hearted old gentleman, before they had time to say a word.

When Clarence left N— — — he was quite sanguine as to his prospects of getting a situation. He carried in his pocket a precious bit of paper, given him by his late employer, Dr. Barrett, which read as follows:

"The bearer of this is an honest, industrious boy, and deserving of any kindness that may be shown him.
"H. M. Barrett, M. D."

That he, Clarence Burton, should ever possess such a document had been far from his thoughts at one time. And it was partly this that made him feel, as the train sped along, that no place on earth had any difficulties that he could not surmount.

Another thing that gave him confidence was the fact that he was going to a new place, amid new scenes, and among new people — people who did not know him as "old Jim Burton's boy."

He felt that he had the same chance to succeed now that any other respectable, ambitious boy had, and this made him feel particularly hopeful.

But when he found himself, with his small bundle, fairly adrift in the busy streets of the city of L— — —, and when he had inquired at several stores for work, and had been told that "no help" was "wanted," he began to realize that it was not such an easy thing to get "a place," even where people knew nothing about him except what his recommendation told them.

For more than a week he walked about, trying place after place, but no work could he get except an occasional horse to hold or a message to carry. In this way he managed to earn enough from day to day to pay for a bed in some cheap lodging house and to buy a bit of bread and cheese.

One morning, as he was walking slowly and disconsolately along a busy thoroughfare, looking wistfully in at the doors of the stores, a gentleman in a large wholesale shoe establishment called to him: "Here, boy, take this letter and mail it for me"; at the same time adding, "Mind, be careful and don't lose it; that's an important letter."

"I'll be careful, sir," answered the boy, promptly running off on his errand.

He was back almost in a moment, and asked the gentleman if he did not "want a boy."

"Well, yes; I believe we do," he answered, giving him, at the same time, a trifle for doing the errand.

"If you want a boy, sir, I'd be very glad if you'd try me," said Clarence, eagerly.

"Have you a recommendation?"

"Yes, sir," answered the boy, proudly, pulling the oft-read bit of paper from his pocket and handing it to his questioner.

"'Honest and industrious,' eh? That's what you are?" said Mr. Emory, who was senior partner of the firm of Emory, Craig & Co.

"I try to be, sir" answered Clarence, modestly.

"Well, do you succeed pretty well?" asked Mr. Emory, looking at him with a twinkle in his eye.

"I think I do, sir," said the lad, looking rather puzzled, and wondering if this was the usual way in which boys were questioned who applied for work in stores.

"All right, then; I'll try you for a while, at any rate. Here, John," called the gentleman to a young man who was passing, "I've a new boy for you; take him and show him what he's to do." And so it was settled, to the great delight of Clarence.

And now life seemed to the boy to have commenced in real earnest.

He was fortunate enough to find a cheap but respectable boarding place, where he could have a room to himself. True, it was the back attic: but what did he care for that, so long as he could be undisturbed? He thought often about his sister and the letter he had promised to send her, but as he had had no good news to tell, he had been unwilling to write. He intended to do so, however, when he was installed in his new situation, but delayed still until he should be *well* settled; and so the days rolled by, and the letter was not written.

Then, too, he had found his way to a night school, and this, with his duties during the day, really left him but little time to be otherwise employed.

When he did write, his letter found Corinne in the worst of her illness, and the letter which had been brought by Miss Rachel was laid aside, with hardly a glance, by Helen. She was too busy and anxious to think about Clarence or any one else, just then; and as for Corinne, she was delirious the best part of her time. She called for her brother; she lived over again her life in the cottage; then she was with Miss Rachel; again she would repeat over her favorite text, "Casting all your care upon him; for he careth for you."

Clarence, of course, knew nothing of all this. He wondered because he received no answer to the letter that had cost him so much pains to write, for he was no skilled penman.

He thought, however, that Miss Rachel Penrose, whom he knew did not entertain the most friendly feelings in the world toward him, had intercepted the letter. He was sure that Corinne had not received it.

"Never mind," he would say to himself; "I'll have Corrie all to myself, some day. But," he would add, wistfully, "I'd like so much to hear from her."

He gave his employers no cause to regret having taken him into the store. Quick, obliging, and polite, he seldom received a sharp word.

He was no special favorite, though, with the boys with whom he came in contact, either about the store or at his boarding place, which was fortunate for him. They found him altogether too economical to suit their fancy, so they contented themselves with calling him names and poking fun at him, all of which Clarence endured good-naturedly. He never refused to do any of them a good turn when it was in his power to do so, but steadily refused to join them in their nightly frolics, he preferring, after his work was done, to go to his humble quarters, eat his supper, tidy up, and go to his beloved night school, where he was doing well with his studies.

And so the winter passed, and still he heard nothing from Corinne. At last he gave up looking for a letter from her, and settled down with the determination to work as hard as he could and save as much of his modest earnings as he was able after keeping himself supplied with plain, comfortable clothing, and paying his board. His wages were small, and the reader may guess that his pile of savings did not grow very fast. However, he was made out of the stuff that was bound to succeed if there was any such thing as success to be found.

Very differently was the time passing with Corinne, whom we left in the midst of the fever which came so near depriving her of life.

Never had child more faithful nurses and nursing than had this orphaned girl.

While Helen was forced to be absent during the day, attending to her school duties, Mary was at home, and, strange to say, seemed in better health than she had been for a long time.

Instead of giving way under the strain of nursing the sick child every day, she seemed to gain strength.

When Helen came home in the afternoon, she relieved her sister entirely, sitting up nearly every night while Mary took needed rest. Dr. Barrett was as attentive to the little waif as he could have been to the child of the most high-born lady in the land; and, really, it would have been very ungrateful in Corinne if she had not pulled through after all the care she had.

CHAPTER IX
The Letter

Miss Rachel Penrose had been, once or twice, to see the little girl, when the fever was at its height, and had been much dismayed at the turn things had taken. She declared that she couldn't, for the life of her, tell what made the child sick. She was "sure it wasn't the little bit of work she did"; she was equally sure that it was "not for want of proper food"; and as for religious training, she was satisfied that she had had the best.

Helen said nothing to all this, but looked indignant.

Miss Rachel kept on with a self-satisfied air: "A body never gets any thanks for raising other folks' children. What with the worry and bother of teaching *them* to work as didn't know clean from dirty; and the toil of making *them* read the Bible as was little better than heathen," she'd "had enough."

"Suppose, then, you give Corinne to me, in case she should recover," suggested Helen.

"I've a good mind to do it," replied Miss Rachel, coolly; "but there's her victuals and clothes as I've found her. I'll lose all that; not to say anything about the trouble I took a-showing her how to do things."

This was more than Helen could stand, and her eyes sparkled angrily as she said, as calmly as she could: "I should say that the child had done enough, since she came to you, to more than pay you for what you have given her, to say the least — — —."

What more she would have said was not said to Miss Rachel; for she hastily interrupted her with: "Well, well, we'll say no more about it. If you want the girl, you're welcome to her. I hope, though, you'll be better paid than I was." And, without giving Helen time to say anything else, Miss Rachel took her leave. This was the last time she came to see them.

At length, after weeks of suffering, Corinne was pronounced by the doctor to be out of danger; and when she awoke from the deep sleep that marked the crisis in her illness, there was quiet, but genuine rejoicing among the three faithful watchers.

At first Corinne was too weak to do anything but smile, and even the smile was a pitiful little ghost of a smile; but gradually her strength began to return, but so slowly that it was very plain to see that it would be long before she would regain even so much as she had when she was first taken ill.

One afternoon, as Helen sat beside her, she heard her name spoken softly; and, looking up from the book she was reading, she saw the dark eyes of the sick child fixed upon her with a troubled expression in them.

"What is it, Corinne?" she asked, smiling.

"Have I been sick ever since that Sunday?"

"Yes, dear; you have been ill ever since then. But why do you ask?"

"I'm afraid I've been a great deal of trouble," said the child.

"It doesn't matter what you've been, except you've been very sick. We kept you our own selves. You had nothing to do with it at all. So don't go and fret, and make yourself worse; there's a good girl. Just drink this beef tea, and go to sleep again. The doctor says you must try and get strong."

The last was said because Corinne had shaken her head at the beef tea. However, she took it; and then, after a minute's silence, said: "But Miss Rachel — — —."

"Oh, she's all right," interrupted Helen. "You're not to go back to live with her any more."

"I'm so glad," said the child. And she drew a long breath of relief. Then, with a happy smile on her face, she soon fell fast asleep.

After this she regained strength more rapidly, but *still* not so fast as Dr. Barrett could wish, as he told her when he came to pay his last professional visit. But, he said, he supposed he must have patience. So, promising to look after her once in a while in a friendly way, the good doctor climbed into his buggy and drove off.

He had another boy to look after Ned, who was not quite so troublesome as formerly. The boy was Clarence's old acquaintance, Tom Greene, who, Dr. Barrett declared, was off at marbles, or something else, every time his back was turned. But it was the best that could be done. A boy he was obliged to have; "and," as he remarked to Corinne one day, "all boys are not like your brother Clarence, my dear." These words made Corinne feel very proud of her brother. They also aroused anxious thoughts as to what had become of him.

These thoughts she kept to herself, however, as long as she could. But one evening, as the three were sitting together, Helen noticed that Corinne looked as if something was on her mind.

"Why do you look so sad, Corinne?" she asked.

The child looked up, hesitated for an instant, and then said: "I was thinking how strange it was that I haven't heard from Clarence."

"Oh, Corinne!" exclaimed her friend, rising hastily, and going to the place where she had put the letter which had come while the little girl was ill; and taking it from its hiding place between the leaves of a book, she handed it to Corinne, who received it with an exclamation of delight.

"Why, Helen," said Mary, in surprise, "when did that letter come?"

"I'm so sorry; it came while Corinne was so very sick. She was delirious at the time; and, of course, I didn't give the letter a thought, but laid it away, intending to give it to her when she got better."

"Poor Corrie!" said Mary, patting the thin hand that rested in the child's lap, with the precious letter held tightly between the fingers.

"Poor Corrie! It wasn't at all certain that she would get better at all, was it?"

"No, indeed," replied her sister, gravely. "It was almost a miracle that she did."

Corinne opened her letter with trembling fingers, and tried to read it; but soon gave up the attempt, and gave it to Helen, asking her to read it for her, which she did. The letter told her how Clarence had tried so long to get work without success, and how at last he succeeded. It told too about his boarding place, and the night school;

how he was saving all he could; and wound up with a repetition of the plans that were to be carried out some time in the future.

"Why, Corinne," said Helen, when she had finished reading the letter, "Clarence tells you to be sure and send him a letter, and doesn't tell you where to send it. How careless of him!"

"And he wouldn't get a letter if I should send him one, would he?" asked Corinne, anxiously.

"I'm afraid not," was the answer.

"A letter might be sent to him in the care of his employer," observed Mary.

"Yes, but Clarence does not give the name of his employer," answered her sister.

"That is too bad," said Mary. Then, seeing the tears gathering in Corinne's eyes, she hastened to say: "Don't cry, Corrie. You can send him a letter, anyway; maybe he'll get it from the post-office. He may see it advertised, you know." And Corrie was comforted.

In due time the letter, telling Clarence of his sister's illness, was written and sent, but failed to reach him.

It was not until Corinne was beginning to seem a little more like herself that the sisters allowed the thought of what was to be done with her to intrude itself. Much as they would have liked to give the little girl a home with themselves, they knew that they could not do so. At the same time they could not bear to send her away from them unless they could find her a better home than she had had with Miss Rachel Penrose.

They did not speak of these things to Corinne. She was so sensitive — so unlike a child. They knew that it would make her unhappy if she even imagined that she was a burden to them; and she seemed so thoroughly to enjoy the quiet, peaceful life of their home, that it was not to be wondered at that they should be reluctant to say anything that would disturb her.

"And, anyway, it would do no good to say anything to her about it, Mary," said Helen. "We wouldn't do anything but keep her until we find a good home for her. So we'll just wait."

There was one thing that worried Corinne a good deal, and that was, that Clarence knew nothing of the new hope that she possessed, and which made her feel so happy. This was especially so because, as she said to Mary one day, when they had been reading and talking about these matters, "Clarence never cared for such things. I wish he would."

"Maybe he will, some day," was the gentle answer.

"We must pray for him."

"I do," replied Corinne.

"Then you must trust. 'All things are possible with God,'" quoted her friend.

"I know that, Miss Mary; and I'm so glad they are."

"You love the dear Lord a great deal, don't you, Corrie?"

"Yes, indeed," answered the child, eagerly. "How could I help it, Miss Mary, when he has been so good to me?"

"'The Lord is my Shepherd, I shall not want,'" repeated her companion, in sweet, reverential tones. "'He maketh me to lie down in green pastures; he leadeth me beside the still waters. He restoreth my soul; he leadeth me in the paths of righteousness, for his name's sake. Yea, though I walk through the valley of the shadow of death, I will fear no evil; for thou art with me. Thy rod and thy staff they comfort me.'"

"That was very sweet, Mary dear," said Helen, who had entered the room unobserved. "I always did love that Psalm."

"Yes," replied her sister, dreamily. "I think it is beautiful."

CHAPTER X

Clarence's Adventure

"I wonder why Corrie doesn't answer my letter. It has been months since I sent it; but I don't wonder much, either, for I don't believe that Miss Rachel would give it to her if it fell in her hands; she never did like me, anyway."

Clarence did not know that the reason he had received no letter was because he had failed to tell his sister where to send one. Nor could he know that Corinne had written, even though she did not know his address, and so he knew nothing of the little girl's illness.

The boy was doing well, and had grown to be quite a different-looking boy from what he was when he first came to L— — —.

He had given his employers perfect satisfaction, having taken pains to please them. Indeed, he was a favorite with nearly everybody about the store.

There was one boy, however, who was also employed there, whose name was Sam Baker, who entertained any other than friendly feelings toward him; and it was the very fact that Clarence was a favorite that caused Sam to dislike him. He called him "stuck up," and "gentleman Clarence," and said a great many ugly things to and about him, to all of which Clarence paid as little attention as possible.

With the exception of Sam's petty annoyances, he had no cause to complain. True, he was not accumulating money as fast as he could have wished, but he had been benefited in many other ways by his life in L— — —, and the old life had become almost like a disagreeable dream, and would have been entirely forgotten but that Corinne was still connected with it.

One dark, rainy night in March, as he was walking home from night school, which had kept in much later than usual, something prompted him to go by the store and see if all was as it should be.

At first he paid no attention to the "notion," as he termed it; but, try as he would, he could not get rid of the feeling that he ought to go, and at length he turned out of his way several squares in order to reach the street upon which the store was situated.

As he approached, he fancied that he saw lights inside. Cautiously advancing and secreting himself in the doorway, he waited and listened.

Yes, he plainly heard voices within; and every now and then caught a glimpse of a dim light flitting here and there.

Swiftly and noiselessly, down the street, went Clarence in search of an officer, and, as it almost always seems in such a case, he thought he never would find one. But at last his search was rewarded, and he rapidly told his story.

The officer summoned help, and together the three repaired to the store. As they neared the building two men and a boy were seen to come out of the door and, without looking behind them, make off as fast as they could.

The officers and Clarence gave chase. When the culprits found that they had been discovered, they separated at the first corner they came to—one keeping straight ahead, the other two taking the cross street.

The officers, intent on catching the men, called to Clarence to "catch the boy."

After a pretty good chase he managed to do so; but what was his astonishment, when he seized the boy's arm, to find that it belonged to Sam Baker.

Indeed, he was so astonished that he forgot to hold it tightly, so that young hopeful had little difficulty in jerking it from his grasp, and, hissing through his teeth, "Tell, if you dare!" disappeared down another street.

Clarence was so dumbfounded that he could not move for a while. When he did, there was nothing to be seen of Sam.

Turning, slowly he retraced his steps. As he went, he was overtaken by another policeman, who had been sent to see what damage had been done at the store. He told Clarence as they walked along together, that the two men had been caught, and in his turn he told the whole story over—how he came to find out about the thieves and how the boy had escaped him, not mentioning, however, that he knew who he was.

It was found, on reaching the store, that the door was unlocked, and in it was a key, showing how the men had entered. Clarence was confident that Sam Baker had furnished them with the key. How it came into his possession he could not tell, and he took care to keep his suspicions to himself. That the men were thieves was apparent, for they had attempted to break open the safe. But either the task had proved too much for them or they had been startled while attempting it. At any rate, they had left without accomplishing their purpose, leaving the key in the lock in their haste.

After what they considered a pretty thorough search, the policemen and Clarence were about to leave the place, having found no serious damage done, when the boy observed that he smelled something burning.

This entailed another search, and, sure enough, they found that a lighted match had been thrown among a pile of rubbish in the cellar; whether purposely or not, they could not tell.

Fortunately, the fire had been discovered before it had gained any headway, and was soon extinguished.

When they were sure that all was entirely safe, the two left the building, the officer locking the door and taking charge of the key.

Clarence, now thoroughly tired out, made his way home as quickly as he could. But he could not sleep after retiring for thinking about the events of the night. He was sorely puzzled too as to what was the best thing to do in the case of Sam Baker. If he told Mr. Emory that he was connected with the attempted robbery, the boy would certainly be turned away, if nothing worse. If he did not tell, might not Sam, finding that he had come off so easily, do something of the same character again? Clarence had heard the boy say that he was nearly all the support his mother had, for she was a widow and in feeble health. This made him very unwilling to do anything that would deprive her of this much-needed help.

He was not sure that he was right in doing so, but he determined, for the sake of Sam's mother, to say nothing about his share in the night's adventure. Having come to this conclusion, he turned over and fell asleep.

There was a great commotion the next morning at the store when it became known what a narrow escape it had from both robbery and fire, and our friend Clarence was fairly lionized when it was found that he had been the means of averting both misfortunes.

The men who had attempted the robbery were found guilty of having committed other depredations, and had been dealt with accordingly. Strange to say, they had said not a word about Sam Baker, and as Clarence had determined to keep his counsel also, no one knew that he was in the remotest way connected with the affair.

Instead of being grateful for having escaped the punishment he so richly deserved, knowing that Clarence could have brought it upon him had he so pleased, Sam was filled with anger at the unoffending boy, which was fanned to still greater heat by the praise bestowed upon him by his employers, and he determined never to rest until he had placed Clarence in a position that would prevent even the possibility of his ever telling of him.

It was not very long before the opportunity he desired presented itself, and it did so after this fashion:

One day it happened that Mr. Emory was in the office, sitting at his desk counting a roll of bills. Clarence, no longer errand boy, was at another desk near by, casting up some accounts. In recognition of the valuable service he had rendered on that rainy March night, the boy had been promised by his friend Mr. Emory, who had been favorably impressed with him from the first, that he should be promoted to the position of assistant clerk if he would hurry up and prepare himself to perform the duties that would be required of him.

The boy had made such good use of his time in night school and on holidays, etc., that, with the aid given him by the other clerks and sometimes by Mr. Emory himself, he hoped to be able to fill this coveted position before a great while.

So very anxious was he to fit himself for it, that he studied and worked during dinner time, just allowing himself a few minutes to snatch a hasty lunch.

It was the noonday hour now, and no one was in the office but himself and Mr. Emory.

Presently the door opened, and a gentleman was shown in by Sam Baker, who had also a message to deliver.

Mr. Emory carelessly dropped the bills he was counting upon the desk, and went toward the gentleman with his hand extended. Having shaken hands, the two were soon earnestly engaged in conversation.

Sam had noticed the bills drop from Mr. Emory's hand, and now, while waiting that gentleman's leisure to attend to him, he slowly edged his way across the room, unnoticed, to the desk, lifted the bills from it, and slipped them into the pocket of the unsuspecting Clarence, who had been so busy with his figures as to not notice the entrance of the new comers further than to raise his eyes an instant when they first entered the room.

He thought that Sam was simply looking over his shoulder to see what he was doing; so he paid no attention to him, but kept on with his work.

Just then Mr. Emory, looking up, saw Sam, and called to him to know if he was waiting for anything.

Baker delivered his message, and left the office well pleased with his work, while Mr. Emory resumed his interrupted conversation, and Clarence steadily plodded on with his accounts, all unconscious of what was in store for him.

At length the visitor took his leave and Mr. Emory returned to his desk, for the first time since leaving it thinking of his money.

CHAPTER XI
Corinne's Journey

The winter had passed, and still no prospect of a new home for Corinne.

The little girl had never fully recovered from her severe illness. The fever had left her very languid. Indeed, the winter proved a trying one to the entire little household.

Mary, never strong, had in some way contracted a heavy cold, which had caused her great discomfort, and seemed to have made serious inroads upon her feeble constitution. She was, therefore, a source of loving anxiety to the sister, who dreaded the least change in the gentle girl's condition, fearful that it might be a forerunner of what Dr. Barrett had warned her would happen some day, that her beloved sister would slip away from her.

Spring had now come, and the doctor had told her that if she possibly could do so, she must take the invalid somewhere where the summer weather would be less oppressive than in N———; for, he said, he did not think Mary could survive the heated term in her feeble condition.

Helen determined, at all hazards, to do everything possible to keep her sister with her, had, with the good doctor's direction, chosen a suitable place, where they could make their home with a relative of his. He was sure too that Helen could obtain a situation as teacher there, and had written about it.

But what was to be done with Corinne? It was out of the question to take her with them, much as they would like to do so; for, aside from the fact that they really had not the means to keep the child, her health was in such a condition as to make it a matter of doubt whether she would ever be really well again; and, as Dr. Barrett said: "Helen already has one invalid to nurse and if she were to have two, she might take it into her head to furnish a third, and then who would do the nursing?"

While this was said in joking tones, it was evident that he was really solicitous for the health of his young friend.

Corinne had endeared herself to the sisters by her gentle, winning ways, and they were loth to part with her under any circumstances, and entirely unwilling to leave her in any but good hands.

The child knew nothing of their difficulties; she only knew that she loved her friends dearly, and endeavored to show her affection in every way in which her willing but weak little hands could. This was about how things stood, when, one Saturday morning, the postman brought Helen a letter.

"Whom is it from?" asked Mary, from her sofa where she lay nearly all the time now.

"I'm sure I don't know, dear," replied her sister, turning it about in an absent sort of way.

She had been looking at the invalid's pinched features, and thinking how much thinner she had grown. And the dread of losing her, and of being left entirely alone in the world, with no one to work for and watch over, was at her heart, and she really did not care to open the letter at all. It was, most likely, of little importance, she thought.

Mary, seeing that Helen seemed low-spirited, and guessing why, asked again where the letter was from, wishing to divert her thoughts.

"It's from Aunt Anna Stone, I think; it's postmarked 'Brierton.'" And Helen slowly opened the envelope.

Aunt Anna Stone was their dead father's half-sister, and it was at her home, "Sweetbrier Farm," that Helen and Mary had spent a part of the previous summer. After rapidly scanning the contents of the letter, Helen lifted her face, her dark eyes bright with the light of a new thought.

"Mary dear, I have it exactly! The very home for Corinne will be with Aunt Anna Stone."

"Did she say so?" asked Mary, archly, smiling at her sister's decided tone.

"Certainly not; how could she, when she doesn't even know that there is such a girl in the world as Corinne? But I mean to write and tell her all about the dear child, and I'm almost certain she'll take her. I wonder why we didn't think of it before." And Helen seated herself at her little desk and began her letter immediately.

She told in her most eloquent manner the story of the poor, homeless child, and asked if it could be so arranged that she might have a home at Sweetbrier Farm. The letter was duly sent, and brought back a speedy reply, to the effect that Corinne would be gladly received, adding, that if the little girl proved to be all she was represented to be, she should be reared by Aunt Anna as her own child. "We can well afford it, Nathan and I," the good woman went on to say; "for while we are but plain country folk, we have enough and to spare. Send the child to us."

"God's way once again!" said Helen, after reading the cordial letter aloud.

"Yes," answered Mary, with her ever ready smile; "isn't it strange how we will try to make ways for ourselves, no matter how often our ways fail; and no matter how many times his ways prove best?"

"Yes, dear, we are very frail creatures."

Corinne did not seem overjoyed at the prospect of having a new home, because she knew she would be obliged to part from the friends who had been so kind to her, and to whom she was so strongly attached. Still, as was usual with her, she said but little.

Helen talked to her a great deal about Brierton and Sweetbrier Farm, describing them and Aunt Anna Stone to the best of her ability, making them all as attractive as possible, for she knew that the child would feel reluctant to go again among strangers.

The days passed rapidly and busily, and at length the time arrived when the little family was to be broken up.

Helen, in the kindness of her warm heart, had denied herself much, in order that Corinne might make her appearance at Brierton in a creditable manner.

The little girl was to make the journey—which was not a long one—alone. And now all was ready. The sisters were to leave N — — — the day following her departure. Corinne strove hard to hide how much she dreaded the separation.

The future looked very dreary to her, especially with the memory of her last home still fresh in her mind. But, child though she was, she was by no means unobservant, and could see that her presence laid an additional burden upon the shoulders of her dear friends. She also saw how they tried to conceal this fact from her, and she felt that, not for the world, would she have murmured once against relieving them.

When the hour of parting came, she bravely bade Mary good-bye, striving hard to keep back the tears, that in spite of all her efforts *would* fall when the gentle girl drew her face down and kissed it, bidding her "be a good girl, and try hard to get well and strong, and be happy," at the same time putting into her hands a small Testament, saying: "Read it often, dear; you will find it a great comfort. I have marked your favorite text, and written it, too, on the fly-leaf. See!"

"'Casting all your care upon him; for he careth for you,'" read Corinne, in a faltering voice.

"Yes, that's it. I love that verse as much as you do. It's so nice to know that we have some one to care for us, and on whom we may cast our care." Then she bade her good-bye again, and Corinne joined Helen, who was waiting for her outside.

She had never been on the cars but once, that was when she first came to N — — — with her father, mother, and brother. Often, in the old days, had she and Clarence stood by and watched the trains rolling in and out, and wished themselves in one of them.

And now that she had the opportunity that she had been so anxious for, she wished it had never come; and yet, at the same time, she felt a mingled feeling of half-fearful and pleasant anticipation at the thought of riding behind the great iron thing that was now puffing and snorting as if impatient at being obliged to wait on the puny creatures gathered about awaiting the signal for starting.

Helen led Corinne to a seat, made her comfortable, kissed her good-bye, slipped into her hand a little purse, then hurried out of the car, none too soon. As the train moved off she waved her hand and smiled at the forlorn little face at the window.

Corinne watched the beloved figure, standing there in the sunlight, until she could no longer see it, and then she leaned back in her seat, and did her very best to keep from crying outright. Presently the pleasant sensation of riding in the car drove from her mind for a while the thought that she had just parted from her dear friends, perhaps forever.

She looked about her curiously. The passengers were all intent upon their own affairs. Then she turned her attention to the outside, and watched the trees and fields, as they flew by. At first she did not like to find herself flying through the country so fast; but gradually she became very much interested in the flying panorama, and watched with admiring eyes the woods, with their green trees; the fields, with their wild flowers and fresh grass; the brooks, flowing by over their beds of stones, and the ponds, with the great lily leaves lying upon their surface. Everything looked so beautiful, Corinne thought, that she could look, and look forever, without being weary. But, by-and-by, she did get a trifle tired. Helen had given the little girl in charge of the conductor, who was to see that she was put off, with her valise, at Brierton Station.

While it was not a long ride, it had seemed quite long enough to Corinne, who was entirely unused to traveling. Her feet would not walk straight when she first got off the cars; and when she found herself standing on the platform of the little station, and the train moving off, she felt as if *she* was moving instead of the cars.

Helen had written Mrs. Stone what time to look for Corinne, but either she had not received the letter, or had been mistaken as to the time of the train's arrival; at any rate, there was no one there to meet the child. Of course, she did not know which way to turn, and she felt very miserable.

CHAPTER XII

Clarence In Trouble

"Clarence," said Mr. Emory, "did you see anything of a roll of bills on my desk?"

"No, sir," answered the boy, looking up for a moment and then going on with his work.

"Why, that is strange. I had those bills when Mr. Rowell came in. I was counting them and dropped them to talk to him, and now they are gone. Clarence, you must have seen them."

"No, sir," repeated Clarence, looking up again. Then, seeing Mr. Emory look at him a little distrustfully, he exclaimed, indignantly: "You don't think I have your money, Mr. Emory, do you? Here, sir, are my pockets; you can see for yourself." And he turned his pockets inside out; but alas, poor boy! From the last pocket there dropped the missing bills.

For a minute neither spoke. Mr. Emory was silent from surprise and disappointment, Clarence from dismay and perplexity.

His employer was the first to break the silence, and then he only uttered the word "Clarence!" but there was a world of significance in that one word, and Clarence felt it keenly and it made him wince; but what could he say? There were the bills, and he felt within himself: "What will be the use of saying I didn't take them? There they are, and who'll believe me if I do say so?" Nevertheless, he did say: "I did not take the money, Mr. Emory."

It seemed as if a mountain of care had fallen upon him in those few minutes, and there he stood — for he had risen — without another word to say.

"Clarence," said Mr. Emory, in sad but firm tones that said as plainly as could words, "It's no use to deny anything"; "Clarence, I'm sorely disappointed in you. But for your past conduct and the kindly feeling I have had for you heretofore I would have you arrested. As it is, I wish you to leave me immediately; and never let me see you again. And you may be thankful you get off so easily. Go!"

Clarence started, but stopped at the door and, turning, said in a low but steady voice:

"Mr. Emory, I am going, and you shall not see me again; but I want to say once more, before I go, that I did not put those bills in my pocket."

"Oh, of course not! they got in there themselves," returned the gentleman, sneeringly.

Clarence, trembling now with anger, hurried out and closed the door.

"Thief!" said a low voice, as he passed somebody at the door. "Who stole the bills?" It was Sam Baker, who chuckled with glee as his victim paused and said, in a choking voice: "Yes, you are more than a thief, and you know it!" Then, without trusting himself to say more, the unfortunate boy hastened away.

Sam did not care for what Clarence said; he was only too much pleased to think that his evil works would now be free from the possibility of discovery—at least, so far as Clarence was concerned.

From the scene of some of his happiest as well as his most unhappy moments, the unhappy boy went as fast as his feet could carry him. Straight to his boarding place he went, gathered together his clothes, made them into a bundle, carefully placed in his bosom the old handkerchief in which was tied his little hoard of savings, first taking out, however, what he owed his landlady for board. That good woman was a busy, hard-working body, with no time to waste on her lodgers further than to attend to their wants, but she was really sorry to lose her boy boarder.

"He was such a quiet lad," she observed to the girl who washed the dishes and ran on errands. "I wonder what made him leave so suddint," for Clarence had gone without saying anything further than "good-bye," and that he was "never coming back any more."

"Perhaps he stole," remarked the maid, with a sage look.

"Stole! not he," cried the good woman, indignantly. "He'd no more steal than you would—not nigh so soon," she added.

"Mis' Tabb, you wouldn't dare say as ever I stole!" retorted the girl, with a defiant toss of the head, at the same time casting a side glance at her mistress to see if she looked as if she suspected anything.

"Mis' Tabb," however, simply gave her shoulders a little shrug and went out of the room, leaving her maid in a rather uncomfortable state of mind, for "there's no tellin's what she knows or don't know, she's so queer like," she muttered to herself.

When Clarence turned from the door of the house that had been a home to him for months, he kept right on without knowing or caring where he was going; his only thought was to get as far away from the scene of his trouble as he could.

Oh, what a crowd of conflicting thoughts were whirling through his brain! His head ached with their pressure.

"Alone again! Forsaken again! Despised again! What's the good of trying to do or be anything? I was born to be downtrodden—crushed!"

These were some of the thoughts that nearly drove him wild.

At last he stopped, simply because he was too tired and weak to go farther. He sank down on a doorstep and buried his face in his hands, and burst into tears and sobbed violently. He wept until his tears were exhausted, and then he laid his poor, tired, aching head upon his arm on the sill of the door and, sitting thus, fell fast asleep.

How long he slept he did not know, but he was awakened by some one shaking him.

He opened his eyes and saw a pleasant-faced, motherly looking old woman standing near.

"What are you doing here, boy?" she asked, putting down a large, heavy basket which she was carrying.

Thinking that she lived in the house on whose doorstep he had been sleeping, he arose, and in his wretchedness, hardly knowing what he did, exclaimed in defiant tones:

"Yes, drive me away from here. I'm a poor dog, and haven't even a right to rest on a doorstep! I wonder if there's a corner in the world where I may lie down and die."

"Hush, boy!" said the old woman. "You are very wicked to talk like that." And she put her wrinkled hand on his shoulder and bade him tell her what was troubling him.

Her kind tones encouraged and comforted poor Clarence, and before he knew it he was pouring out the story of his woes into her listening and sympathizing ears.

He told her everything, and ended with: "I never could be content to be a vagabond and a good-for-nothing, but there's no chance for me, no matter how much I want to do right and be somebody; there's always something that comes and crushes me down; and now I'm entirely discouraged."

"Ah! but, my boy, that's not right," said his new friend, soothingly. "If you are down, there's one above that can lift you up."

Without heeding her, the boy continued, bitterly:

"When I lived in the old place I made up my mind to go off, and but for my sister I'd have done it; but for her sake I stayed, and then our mother must die and our father must leave us to be turned out into the street. Then I came here, and walked, and walked, until I was ready to drop before I could get a place, and just as I thought I had a good chance to come up, I must be called a thief and be driven away like a dog. No; I'll look for no more chances. I don't care what becomes of me."

"Boy," said the old woman, solemnly, "I say again that you are very wicked to talk that way. None of us can have things just as we want them in this world; and it isn't best that we should. Don't you know that our ways are in God's hands? He rules things for us as it pleases him, whether it suits us or not. Boy," she asked, gravely, "are you one of his children?"

Clarence had calmed down now, and it was in subdued tones that he answered: "I'm afraid not, ma'am."

"Well, you ought to be; and you must be. Promise me that you will."

"How can I promise you that when I'm wicked? You said yourself that I was wicked."

"Well, so you are; but you're not so wicked that he won't forgive you if you want him to, and ask him. You can do that, can't you?"

"Yes," said Clarence, slowly; "I guess I can; and I will, if you think it will do any good."

"That's right. Of course it will do good. But where are you going? You can't stay here all the time."

"I don't know where to go. I don't want to go anywhere," answered the boy, the thought of his lonely condition coming back to him with fresh force.

"Oh, no, that will never do," said his friend. "Suppose you come home with me for a while. You can carry my basket for me, can't you? I can get along faster then."

Clarence was glad enough to accept her kind offer, for he dreaded going in search of another lodging. Eagerly seizing the basket and tossing it on his arm, he signified his readiness to go, adding that he would do anything in the world for his new friend.

The street on which they had held their conversation was a lonely, deserted sort of place, and the house before which they stood, and on the steps of which Clarence had slept, was untenanted, though he did not know it.

He and his companion soon left this quiet neighborhood far behind. For some time they walked on in silence, then Clarence asked, anxiously: "You don't believe I took that money, do you?"

"That I don't, my boy, or I'd never do by you as I am doing," said the good woman, heartily.

Presently they turned into a little, narrow street, lined on either side with small dwellings. About midway, they paused before a tiny shop. Its one window was tidily arranged, and the half-glass door was neatly curtained with white muslin.

Taking a key from her pocket, "Mother Carter," as she was called in the neighborhood, opened the door and led the way into her little domain.

She lived there all alone, supporting herself with the profits of her little trade in groceries, coal and wood, thread, needles and pins, etc.

She was a good, Christian soul, with a kind word and open hand to all who were needy, so far as her ability went.

She was respected and beloved by her neighbors. In her quiet way she ministered to those who were in want, never failing to put in a word or two of either advice, admonition, or comfort, as the case required. It is not always necessary that people should live very prominent and public lives in order to be useful. Lights are burning where the busy world sees them not; but that it does not see or know them does not alter the fact that they are performing their mission. When we are sailing far out upon the ocean, at night we cannot see the lights along the shore; but they are there, just the same, and those near them can see them. So in life, lights dim or bright do not shine without some to see them and be thankful for their shining.

One can be as grateful for a tallow candle, if it is that which gives him light, as another is for the brilliant electric lamp. Each and every one fills a niche in the world, and has usefulness and appreciation. And perhaps that which seems least may at last be found greatest. Motives will measure, and God will judge.

CHAPTER XIII
New Experiences

We left Corinne standing on the platform of the little railway station at Brierton, with the train disappearing in the distance.

"Hello, sis, what 're you waitin' for?" called a boy who had been perched upon a fence near by. While he spoke, he climbed down and came toward the little girl.

Corinne turned and looked at her questioner, and, in spite of her low spirits, she could not help an amused smile which crept over her face, when her eyes fell upon the odd-looking lad who stood before her with his hands in his pockets, and a perfectly self-satisfied expression on his countenance.

His clothing was little other than "rags"; and there was scarcely any form or shape in it. Even his hat was little more than a brim; his head having pushed the little crown it possessed up in a slanting position, through which his thick, rough locks struggled, apparently to free themselves. His black eyes had a mischievous twinkle in them; his face was thin, with high cheek bones; and his whole appearance was grotesque and comical in the extreme.

Corinne's smile did not seem to offend him in the least, but rather pleased him; for he gave an answering grin, and exclaimed, swinging his long, rag-bedecked arms back and forth enthusiastically: "That's the ticket, young 'un. You look heaps better now. What's the use o' lookin' so oncommon glum—just as if you was a goin' to a funeral. Where do you belong, anyway?"

"I'm from N———, and I am to go to Mrs. Stone's" said Corinne. "Do you know where she lives?"

"Mrs. Stone's? Know? Guess I do," jerked out the queer boy. "I can take you there, if you like. But what on earth are you goin' there for?" he added, with more curiosity than good manners.

"I'm going there to live," faltered Corinne.

"Whew!" whistled her new acquaintance. "No wonder your face was a yard and a quarter long. Don't fancy it, eh?"

"I don't know," stammered Corinne. "I never saw Mrs. Stone."

"Oh, you didn't? Why, how funny! What makes you go there, then?"

But Jack's queries were interrupted just here in rather an unceremonious manner by old Robin Joyce, the station master, who, laying a heavy hand upon his shoulder, asked him if it wasn't time he'd taken himself off about his business, if he had any.

"I'm just goin', boss. My business just now is to 'scort this young 'un"—pointing to Corinne—"over to Mrs. Stone's."

"Well, can't you do it wi'out axin' so many questions?"

"Guess I can if I want to," was the saucy answer, given, however, after putting a little space between himself and the old man.

"Come on, young 'un," he called to Corinne, who complied quickly, for she was afraid he would go away and leave her; and she did not know how she would find her destination if he did.

"Won't you bring my valise?" she asked, timidly, putting some money in Jack's grimy hand.

Jack did as he was requested, and then Corinne followed her comical-looking escort, who asked no more questions, but kept ahead of her, walking briskly.

It was a bright, pleasant day, in the latter part of May; but the roads were rough, and Corinne's feet grew very tired, and ached a good deal before they reached the dingy old house where Jack informed her "Mis' Stone lives."

Everything about it looked barren and uninviting. Even the chickens that walked in and out of the broken palings looked dull and ill-natured. A lank, gray cat was stretched out on the front doorstep; but as the visitors approached, it slowly arose, and walked off with an unfriendly air. Jack, who considered himself quite an important personage, gave a loud knock at the door, which had no effect, however, except to awaken echoes.

Again and again he knocked, each time a little louder than before. Just as he was preparing to give another bang, the door opened so suddenly and unexpectedly as almost to disconcert the boy, who was by no means easily startled. A tall, hard-featured woman, who reminded Corinne strongly of Miss Rachel Penrose, stood before them, and demanded what was wanted.

"Mis' Stone, I've brought you some company," quoth Jack, with his ever ready and complacent smile.

"Oh, you have, have you?" returned 'Mis' Stone,' tartly. "Well, you can just take 'em back where you got 'em from." And without more ado she slammed the door, and returned to her work.

Corinne and Jack looked at each other in dismay.

"Well, that's a nice way to treat company!" ejaculated the boy, pulling off his piece of a hat, and rubbing his bushy hair vigorously. "Was she lookin' for you?"

"Yes," said Corinne, faintly. "Miss Helen wrote and told Mr. Stone — — —"

"Mr. Stone!" interrupted Jack. "Why, there ain't any Mr. Stone. He's been dead for years and years."

"Dead!" repeated the sorely puzzled Corinne. "Oh, dear! what *does* it all mean?" And the tears gathered in her eyes. "They told me that Mr. Stone was nice, and Mrs. Stone was nice, and that they lived in a pretty place," said the child.

"Well, don't you call this a pretty place?" asked Jack, putting his head on one side, and looking about with a critical expression.

"As to the missus, now, I don't go to say as she's so very nice; but I say—he!" And Corinne was astonished to see her companion turn a somersault; in the accomplishment of which he still farther damaged his already very much dilapidated hat. Taking it off and carefully patting the crown down, he said: "There, I've spoiled my hat!" with such a rueful countenance that Corinne could not help laughing.

"Oh, yes, you can laugh. But see here; I've brought you to the wrong place. I always thought I had some wits; but if I had, I'm afraid I've lost em, sure's my name's Jack."

"They've gone out through the crown of your hat, maybe,

Jack," said Corinne, finding the boy's good humor contagious.

"Just as like as not," said Jack, solemnly.

"But, Jack, if this isn't the place, where is it? Didn't you say this was Mrs.Stone's?"

"Yes, I did; and so it is. But there's two Mis' Stone's. T'other lives at a place called Sweetbrier Farm."

"Oh, yes," cried Corinne, "that's the place I was to go to. How stupid in me to forget! I'm so glad that this is the wrong place." And Corinne shuddered as she thought of "Mis' Stone." "Is it far to the other place?"

"Far? Guess it is for you. It's two miles."

"Oh, dear!" sighed the weary child. "I couldn't walk so far. I'm so tired."

"Well, now, I reckon that's so, 'cause you don't look strong; but I don't know what else you'll do."

Just then a wagon came jolting along the road, driven by a sleepy-looking man in a broad straw hat and a blue cotton shirt.

"Hey, Mister," called Jack, "can't you give this young 'un a lift as far as Sweetbrier Farm?"

"Reckon so," was the short answer, as the man brought his slow-moving brown mare to a standstill.

"Are you going past there?" asked Corinne, anxiously, afraid of making another mistake.

The man nodded, and motioned her to get into the wagon, which she very willingly did; for she was very much fatigued.

Jack placed her valise beside her; and then, waving his ragged hat, as the wagon moved off leisurely, called: "Good-bye, young 'un." Then away he went, whistling merrily.

Corinne felt really sorry to part with her odd acquaintance. She was so lonely, that any cheerful face was pleasant to meet.

Much as Corinne dreaded to meet strangers, she was glad when the man turned up a tree-shaded lane, and stopped before the gate of a white house. The sound of wheels brought to the door an elderly woman, in a neat print gown and a snowy cap. Corinne knew her to be Aunt Anna Stone, from the description her friends had given of her.

It was a pleasant sight for the tired girl. The clean, cool-looking house, with the bright green of the yard about it, and the lane, with the evening shadows beginning to play about in it now, stretching out toward the broader fields; and then, best of all, the benevolent-looking, friendly woman who stood there to welcome her—to look it as well as to speak it—all this was very delightful to our little waif. It would seem as though a haven of refuge was opening for her at last, and that in it she would find what so much she needed—a home and love.

"Well, now, Jonathan Banks, you don't mean to tell me that that's our little girl you've got there?" the good woman cried, coming forward to meet them.

"Don't know, mum," replied the man, impatient to be off. "It's a gel as axed me to bring her along, bein's I was a-comin' this way."

"Why, my dear," said Mrs. Stone, addressing Corinne, "why didn't the girls write us when you were to come, so that we could have sent some one to meet you? It was too bad for you to have to find your way here all by yourself."

"Miss Helen did write, please, ma'am," said Corinne.

"Did she? Why, that's strange. We didn't get the letter; it must have miscarried. But, anyway, I'm real glad to see you. Come right in." And taking Corinne's hand she led her into the house, having first slipped a piece of money into the hand of Jonathan Banks, who thanked her gruffly, and drove his old mare down the lane and away.

CHAPTER XIV
A Home At Last

I t was just five by the old-fashioned clock in Mrs. Stone's kitchen when she and Corinne entered.

The sun was shining in through the windows, and lighted up the floor and the table set for tea, and danced to and fro on the walls. A wood fire was crackling on the hearth, and the kettle sang merrily.

The room, from its appearance, was evidently used as dining and sitting room, as well as kitchen; and a very pleasant place it seemed to tired little Corinne, whom Mrs. Stone had placed in a low chair by the window to rest. Meanwhile, she set the tea to draw, cut the bread, brought the butter and milk, and, in short, put the finishing touches to the preparations for the evening meal.

When Mr. Stone came in to tea, our little friend was glad to find him as genial and pleasant as his wife. Of course, he too was surprised to find Corinne there. Both Mr. Stone and his wife were pleased with the child's quiet ways and demure looks.

"Come, Corinne, my dear, and get your tea. I know you must be hungry." This was true; for she had eaten nothing since early in the day. So, placing the little stranger between herself and her husband, she began pouring out the tea.

Corinne had dreaded the introduction to her new home, expecting that she would feel strange and alone; but, to her utter surprise, she felt herself as much at home amid her new surroundings as if she had lived there for years.

Tea over, Mr. Stone went out; and Mrs. Stone, with Corinne's help, cleared away the tea things.

The child felt much rested and refreshed after her tea, and quite delighted her new friend with her ready, quick movements. The pure country air was beginning already to benefit her; for, in spite of the trying experiences of the day, she felt stronger and better than she had done for a long time.

After all was done, Mrs. Stone took her work basket and her seat near the window, and began to sew; while Corinne sat on a low stool near the open door.

For a while neither spoke; but silence for any great length of time not having a place in good Mrs. Stone's creed, she soon broke it by asking the little girl a host of questions about her friends Helen and Mary Gray, reciprocating by telling many little incidents of their visit to Sweetbrier Farm, the previous summer.

Corinne was so fatigued with the long, tiresome day, that she fell fast asleep while the good woman was talking.

As twilight was now gathering, and she could not see well to sew, Mrs. Stone began folding up her work. Noticing that the little girl was very quiet, she glanced at her to see why it was.

"Well, well," she said, softly, "if I haven't talked the child to sleep. Now that is too bad. I might have known that she is worn out with traveling, and one thing and another."

She gently waked Corinne, and led her to the little room that she told her was to be her "very own."

Corinne, who was wide awake now, looked about her in pleased surprise. "What a dear little room!" she said, in grateful tones.

"I'm glad you like it, my dear," replied Aunt Anna, as she had told Corinne to call her. She offered to help her; but the little girl thanked her, and said she could manage nicely herself. So Mrs. Stone bade her goodnight, and went down stairs.

When she was left alone, Corinne sat down, and tears of gratitude sprang to her eyes, as she noted the preparations that had been made for her—for *her*, Corinne Burton—who, a short time ago, had none to even so much as speak a kind word to her. She could hardly believe that it *was* Corinne Burton who sat in the little cushioned chair, and looked about at the pretty white bed and neat furniture that were for her use.

As she sat thus and thought over the past, with its many

hardships and discouragements, and on the present, with new and unlooked-for blessings that threw a bright and hopeful light upon the future, the sensitive child was entirely overcome; and, throwing herself upon her knees by her bedside, she sobbed out her gratitude to the Father above, whose guiding hand had led her through hidden paths; and she resolved that, with his aid, she would never let one act of hers bring uneasiness or care to the kind friends whom she already loved dearly.

Rising from her knees, her thoughts turned to the friends she had left; and, taking the little Testament that had been the parting gift of her beloved "Miss Mary" from her pocket, she opened it lovingly at the familiar place, which was marked by a tiny blue ribbon, and a bright smile spread over her features as she read the words she loved so much, and of which she never grew tired: "Casting all your care upon him; for he careth for you." Closing the book, she laid it on the neat bureau. Then, having prepared for rest, she again knelt and prayed that she might be kept through the night; and she prayed for a blessing upon those with whom her lot was cast. Nor did she forget Clarence — poor Clarence! — far away from her, where, she did not know; for she had heard nothing from him since his first letter. She knew nothing of the chequered scenes through which he was passing, but God knew; and none can tell how much her prayers availed for her poor, struggling brother.

Quite refreshed by a good, sound sleep, Corinne awoke bright and early next morning.

It was Sunday, and a lovely day. A holy calm rested upon everything, and the spirit of the day of rest seemed to have entered into nature. The fields, clad in their fresh, bright verdure, lay peaceful in the early morning sunlight, while the trees waved their tender green leaves gently in the soft breeze.

Corinne quickly dressed herself, and then threw open her window, that the yellow sunbeams might shine in. Kneeling beside her bed, as she had done the night before, and as she had not failed to do since she had found out that she had a Father in heaven, to whom she might go at all times, and to whom she was indebted for all the good she received, she offered her morning prayer of thanksgiving to that Father for his protection during the night; adding a petition for help to live aright during the day, as her invalid friend had taught her.

Rising from her knees, she opened her little Testament and read a chapter. This done, she went to the window, and, leaning out, enjoyed keenly the pure air and beautiful scenery which lay before her.

How peaceful it was! What a refreshing stillness brooded over all; and what a feeling of rest came upon the child, as her eyes wandered dreamily from green field to shady wood! Away in the distance, she could trace the line of a stream of water, by the border of low trees that grew on its banks; while the tinkle of cow bells and the occasional crowing of cocks broke what would otherwise have seemed an oppressive quiet.

Truly, on such a morning, and amid such surroundings, it is fitting and natural that the holiest and best thoughts in one should be brought into play; and Corinne's heart swelled with emotion, and her lips could do nothing but murmur thanks to the God who had led her feet through paths she knew not of, to such a haven of rest. Could she "*ever* be grateful enough"? She felt as if she could not.

The strongest wish she had at that moment was to stay forever in this lovely country home. But all dreams must come to an end at some time. So, rousing herself, she went down stairs, where she found Mrs. Stone bustling about.

"Good-morning, my dear," was her greeting. "Isn't this a lovely morning?"

"Indeed it is," answered Corinne, all her timidity dispelled by the genial tones of her kind friend. "Indeed it is. I don't think I ever saw a lovelier."

"Then you like the country" said Aunt Anna, in pleased tones.

"Yes, oh, yes. It is so sweet and quiet. I love it!" And the sparkling eyes and long-drawn breath plainly showed that Corinne spoke truly.

"Now I'm real glad of that." And Mrs. Stone paused in her preparations for breakfast, and looked out of the open door, across the fields. "I love the country too"—her voice taking on a low, reverent tone as she spoke—"it always seems to me as if God and heaven are nearer to us in the country than anywhere else."

"Didn't you always live in the country?" asked Corinne.

"Dear, no, child. I was born and bred in the city. But I came here soon after I was married; and here I've been ever since. But come, now. Wouldn't you like to feed the chickens and ducks this morning?"

"Oh, I should, ever so much," cried Corinne.

"I thought you would," said Aunt Anna. Then, having given her the pan of food, and instructions how to call the fowls together, she went back to her duties; while Corinne, happy as a queen, called about her such a crowd of clucking, cackling, crowing, quaking creatures, as she had never seen together at one time in all her life.

Mrs. Stone loved fowls, and was always fortunate in raising them. She made great pets of them too. Indeed, some were so spoiled that they would jump right up and peck out of the dish as she held it. And such a fine lot as they were! There were stately, handsome cocks, staid, motherly hens, saucy little bantams, and wee balls of baby chicks.

Corinne had never been so perfectly happy before. The healthful air had put new life into her wasted little frame; and the knowledge that she had, at last, a home, filled her heart so full of joy, that she could have shouted right out.

When she had finished her pleasant task, she went into the house with a shy, smiling face, as if she hardly dared smile, lest it should all change—all the pleasant things that had befallen her—into something disagreeable. But no; it was too real to change. Aunt Anna smiled too, when Corinne told her how she had enjoyed feeding the fowls; and then they all sat down to breakfast—not, however, before Mr. Stone, or Uncle Nathan, as Corinne had been instructed to call him, had read a psalm and offered a simple, but earnest petition heavenward.

Corinne helped clear away the breakfast things when the morning repast was finished; and then Aunt Anna said it was time to get ready for church.

It was not far away,—the church which they attended,—and they could see its white, inviting appearance as they looked across the green fields. It was most pleasantly situated, and in itself it seemed a call to prayer to all the country for miles around.

And, for the most part, the people heeded it. Their work was laid aside, and they gathered for worship. Pleasant greetings they exchanged, as they met at the church door, for the work of the week kept them from seeing much of each other at other times. And then they all passed in, and the sounds of the worship within mingled with the sounds of the worship without—the sounds of the rustling in the trees, and the singing of birds, and the humming of bees as they went from flower to flower.

It would be a pleasant scene for our little girl, and thoroughly— as we shall see by-and-by—she enjoyed it. The winter had indeed passed for her, and the time of the singing of birds had come.

CHAPTER XV
Mother Carter

"Now, Clarence, or Clarie, or whatever you call yourself, just stir about and help me get a bit of supper ready. Light up a fire, will you, and set the kettle on, while I lay the table."

All the time she was talking, Mother Carter was busy taking off her bonnet, and putting away her purchases, which were articles for her little shop.

Clarence liked to feel that he was helpful, and soon made himself acquainted with the whereabouts of his hostess' belongings. In a short time he had the fire crackling and sputtering, and the kettle filled with water and on the stove. The frugal meal ready, the two sat down to enjoy it.

Mother Carter's apartments consisted of the little shop, her kitchen, and one bedroom. So she made a bed for the boy in the shop, on the floor, after she had closed for the night; and once more the boy laid him down to rest, with the feeling that he was not quite forsaken.

As he lay there on his humble pallet, after the lights were out and all was still, the words of his new friend came to him: "Are you one of God's children? You ought to be. You must be."

He had never before given any attention to such things; but since he had undergone so many hardships, and had been so wretched, he felt that it must be very pleasant to have something to lean upon—some one to look to who would understand all his needs and wants.

Mother Carter had told him how and where to find this One. "But," he kept saying, "I'm so wicked. I'm so wicked. I've no right to go to him for anything." And so he lay, until he dropped off to sleep.

He arose early next morning, before Mother Carter was awake, opened the shop, put things straight in it, and then made a fire in the kitchen stove. When the good woman made her appearance, the kettle was noisily singing, and the table set for breakfast.

"Well, now, Clarence, you're smart, sure enough," she said, nodding her heard, approvingly. Then, as she began to prepare the breakfast, she said: "See here, now, my boy. You know I sell wood; and I'd be just as glad as anything if you'd step down cellar and bring some up, and pile it under the counter in the shop. Dear! dear!" she continued, as Clarence willingly went to obey, "I just see the lots of help you'll be to me. Why, I've often wished I had a lad to give me a lift once in a while; but I didn't know where to lay my hand on the kind of a boy I wanted—boys are such trials, as a general thing. The thought never came into my head, when I brought you home with me yesterday, that I'd found the very boy I was wishing for. 'All things work together for good to them that love God.' You're not that kind, I'm afraid, my boy." And Mother Carter laid her hand on his shoulder.

"No, but I mean to be; that is, I would be if I wasn't so wicked," stammered he, astonished at his own boldness.

"'Though your sins be as scarlet, they shall be as white as snow,'" quoted the good old woman. "Think of that, my boy; think of that."

As Clarence went back and forth from the cellar to the shop, and from shop to cellar, his thoughts were as busy as his feet and hands. He was contrasting *his* mode of righting things with God's way.

In the first place came the life in the old cottage, where we made his acquaintance, and where he had first known the desire to be something more than a vagrant. *His* way of bringing this about was to run away—not the bravest thing in the world to do, to be sure, and he felt it so now; and for the first time a feeling of shame stole over him as he thought of it. However, this was his idea of setting things right about that time. But the death of his mother, and the events that followed in its train, completely did away with that idea.

Then, he had soon tired of his work at the doctor's. He was

ambitious, and wanted something more stirring than driving and holding "Ned," tending the office, etc. So, when he came to L— — —, and obtained employment in Mr. Emory's establishment, with the prospect of advancement before him, he was delighted, and *his* way was to remain there; but circumstances proved that this was not God's way.

Now, Clarence had thought but little of God; had never cared for Sunday-school or church, and never read the Bible; indeed, there was none in the cottage for him to read, had he been so inclined. He had gone occasionally to Sunday-school, and had heard the story of the Redeemer, and how he came into the world and died that sinners might be saved; but he had listened to it thoughtlessly, as so many others have done and do. It all came to him that day, while in the cellar; and he began to sorely feel the need of that Redeemer, and to repent of his past life. And he knelt right down and prayed, as he had never prayed, and as he had not imagined he could pray. He confessed his sins and asked earnestly to be forgiven, and then and there gave himself to God. Was he happy when he arose? I think — nay, I *know* he was.

Mother Carter could not tell what kept him so long down cellar, and was just about to call him to breakfast, when he made his appearance, with his face so radiant and happy, that the dear old lady felt sure that things had come about just as they really had; and she was not a bit surprised when Clarence told her all about it. But the tears came into her eyes, when he said: "Mother Carter, I'm a different boy from the miserable fellow you picked up on the street yesterday."

"I believe you, my boy," she said, wiping her eyes, "but it's all God's doing. Let us thank him."

"I do," answered the boy. "But where should I be now, if you had not come along and talked to me as you did?"

"It was all the leading of the Heavenly Father, Clarence. Never fail to love him with your whole heart, and serve him with all your might."

"I mean to do my best, Mother Carter," said he, reverently; "for I feel just as grateful as I can be."

"That's right! That's right!" she said in response.

Just then the tinkle of the shop bell notified Mother Carter that she was wanted. When her customers were gone, she and Clarence sat down to breakfast, with contented spirits and happy hearts.

Day after day passed, and found him still faithful to his resolutions, and Mother Carter the same motherly body as ever. A genuine attachment had sprung up between the lonely old woman and the friendless boy, that was a comfort to her and was proving of great help to him. He would not allow her to do anything that he could do himself. He made the fire, tended shop, sawed, split, and put away the wood, keeping the supply under the counter constantly replenished, ran errands, and relieved his benefactress in every possible way. She, in her turn, attended to his boyish wants, and gave him a home. She could not give him money, nor did he ask it. He was thankful to have some place he could consider "home," and some one whom he could call "friend." If the thought did come to him sometimes, when he was obliged to draw upon his little store of savings in order to purchase shoes, or clothes, to wish that he was away at work, where he could make more money, he put it aside, out of affection for the only person in the world, except his sister Corinne, who really cared for him.

He had cause to be very thankful that he had so faithfully followed this course; for one evening, while he was out on an errand, Mother Carter met with a serious accident. There was a trap door in the shop that led to the cellar. This door she had opened in order to go down for something she wanted. Just as she was about to do so the shop door opened, and she went behind the counter to attend to the customer, who was a little boy. As his arms were so full of packages when he turned to go that he could not open the door, Mother Carter came around to open it for him.

A neighbor was passing at the time, and stopped for a few moments to have a little chat. When the woman had passed on, Mother Carter closed the shop door, and forgetting that she had intended to go down into the cellar and had left the trap door open, turned and walked briskly across the floor toward the door leading into the next room; and in the dim light not noticing where she was walking, stepped into the opening and fell to the floor of the cellar, striking her back and head forcibly against the cellar steps.

For a moment she felt stunned, and then tried to rise; but the movement caused her so much pain, that she swooned away.

It had been cloudy all the afternoon; and now, as evening closed in, the rain began to fall.

Clarence had to go a long distance, and his errand kept him some time; so that the lights were twinkling in the houses, as he turned his steps homeward.

CHAPTER XVI

Sunday At Brierton

The little church was, as we have said, only a little way from Sweetbrier Farm, and what a delight it was to walk there, through shady lanes and grassy meadows, taking now and then a "short cut" through the grounds of a friendly neighbor, passing beneath the rustling boughs of the trees in the grove, then out again in the bright, beautiful sunlight. Corinne enjoyed it all keenly. She felt as if she had passed into another world.

As they neared the small but neat frame church, they met little groups of people, all wending their way in the same direction, many of them coming from long distances. Some passed them in buggies, some in wagons, some in clumsy carts, but all intent on going to church.

Our friends entered softly and seated themselves. It was quite early, and for some little time the rustle of new arrivals was heard. When the hour for service arrived, the pastor, a tall, middle-aged gentleman, with benevolence and kindly feeling beaming in his genial countenance, read the opening hymn, which was sung by the congregation, with no accompaniment save the music of the birds outside the open windows.

Charley Reade, the minister's little son, often said that the birds liked to come to church on Sundays, and sing with the people. Whether this was so or not, sing they did, with all the power in their tiny throats.

Mr. Reade took for his text that morning the words: "Humble yourselves, therefore, under the mighty hand of God, that he may exalt you in due time."

This verse was familiar to our little friend, Corinne; for it was the one just before her favorite text, and she had read it often. The sermon was simple, forcible, plain, practical, and was delivered in tones that showed that the speaker's sole aim was to reach the hearts of his hearers, and press home upon them the truths contained in his theme. The earnest attention with which his congregation listened to his words fully attested their interest and evident enjoyment.

The sermon was so simple and plain, that Corinne had no difficulty in understanding it all, and she thoroughly enjoyed it. Then the little church looked so neat and pretty, with its dove-colored walls and dark-brown pews, while through the open windows came the soft, sweet breeze, and the trees that stood around cast shadows of their dancing leaves upon the sunlit crimson carpet and against the wall. It all made a very beautiful picture, Corinne thought.

There was one little girl, about the age of our young friend, who sat near by, and who kept her eyes upon her nearly all the time during the service. It was Bebe Reade, Charley's staid little sister. She had been told by Aunt Anna Stone, with whom she was a great favorite, that Corinne was to come to live with her. "Auntie Stone," as Bebe called her, had also told her the story of Corinne's sad life, and the little maiden was full of sympathy for the child.

She was just the least bit impatient, I am afraid, for the service to be over, so that she might make the acquaintance of the new comer. She was quite attracted by Corinne's sober, sweet face and demure air, and made it up in her mind that she and "Auntie Stone's new little girl" should be fast friends. Her brother Charley had looked too, but decided right away that the "stranger girl" was altogether too quiet to suit him; so he leaned back in his seat and watched a bee which had wandered in at the window, and was hovering over the head of good Deacon Phillips, and buzzing sullenly, as if it had half a mind to sting him.

At last service was over, and Bebe had the opportunity she had wished for, and which she improved by going straight over to Corinne, and reaching out her little hand, said, in her matter-of-fact way: "I'm glad you've come, little girl."

Corinne, somewhat taken aback at such a cordial greeting from a stranger, still had sufficient self-possession to return the friendly squeeze Bebe had given her hand, and as the congregation moved slowly out of the church, Aunt Anna Stone noticed with satisfaction that the two little girls walked out with their arms about each other.

Bebe's mother was dead, and Aunt Patty, a widowed sister of Mr. Reade's, had charge of his little household. The two children, Charley and Bebe, each as different from the other as could be, were both, in their respective ways, good, tractable little people. Charley, aged eleven years, was rather inclined to be mischievous; but, as Aunt Patty was wont to say, there wasn't "a bit of harm in the lad; he's only a healthy, lively boy."

Bebe — Blanche Bernice was her real name, shortened to Bebe, because of the two initial Bs — was by no means averse to a "bit of a romp" with her brother, who was her only companion, for the Reade's lived "up country," to use the expression of the Brierton folk, and had no near neighbors. This was one reason why she had been so glad to hear that Corinne was coming to live with "Auntie Stone," and she had hoped that she would make a nice friend and playmate.

And so it proved to be. Corinne and Bebe were quite confidential by the time the older folks were ready to separate.

"I'll come over to see you just as soon as I can," said Bebe, as the two girls parted, reluctantly.

"Bebe, whatever can you see about that stupid girl to like?" exclaimed Charley, as, seated behind their father and Aunt Patty, in the carryall, they rolled slowly homeward.

"She isn't stupid at all, Charley Reade; and you mustn't say such things about her, for she's my friend," said Bebe, indignantly.

"I wouldn't have her for a friend; I wouldn't speak to her; she's only a pauper; I heard Auntie Stone tell all about her to-day, and she's just nobody at all."

"Charley," said his sister, gravely, "you know very well that you are saying naughty, ugly things, and you ought to be ashamed of yourself. Can she help being what she is? I wouldn't let *that* hinder me from being a friend to any one. The Lord loves poor, friendless people, and so do I; and I love Corinne dearly, and I know Auntie Stone does too, from the way she talks to her. Besides, Charley Reade," continued the little maiden, almost out of breath with indignation and her long speech, "besides, your father has taught you better than to talk that way."

"Oh, ho! 'your father has taught you better!' Just listen to Mistress Reade!" cried Charley, mockingly.

"What's the matter, children?" asked their father, half turning around, and noticing the ruffled looks of the occupants of the back seat.

"Why, papa," began Bebe, while Charley sat up very straight, and looked away across the fields. "Charley has been saying all sorts of rude things about Auntie Stone's little adopted girl; he says she's a pauper, and a whole lot more. And, papa, she's a nice girl; I like her, and want to know her—mayn't I?"

"Certainly, dear, if you're sure she's a nice little girl; and I'm certain she must be, or Mrs. Stone wouldn't have taken her. Charley, my boy," he said, looking reproachfully at that young gentleman, who looked very uncomfortable, "Charley, it isn't like you, to talk in that way."

"Well, but, papa," said the boy, "her father is nothing but a drunkard—I heard Auntie Stone say so—and the girl is just nobody."

"Yes, she is somebody; she is a girl with a soul just like yours, and if she is the child of a drunkard, all the more should you pity and be kind and friendly to her."

Having said this, Mr. Reade returned to his former position, and the two children were silent during the remainder of the drive.

When old Bessie, the sorrel mare, stopped of her own accord in front of the gate of their home, Charley was the first to jump out of the carriage, and without waiting for any one, away he went around the house, as fast as he could. Bebe alighted more slowly and soberly, as did also Aunt Patty, while Mr. Reade drove Bessie to her stable.

Bebe went into the house, and, taking a book, brought her little rocking chair out on the front porch and sat down to read. But she missed her brother, who was always on hand on Sundays to read with her. At last she grew tired of sitting there by herself, so she closed her book and went in search of the missing Charley. She found him sitting on the top of the wood pile. Thinking that he was sulky, she climbed up beside him, all unmindful of her Sunday dress, to talk him into a good humor. But there was no ill-temper in the bright, laughing face he turned to her.

"Bebe," he said, "I *am* just ashamed of myself for being so horrid to-day."

"I think you ought to be, you naughty boy; I'm ashamed of you." And the little girl threw her arm around her brother and gave him a loving squeeze. Then the two sat there without saying any more; but both were busy with their thoughts, and, strange to say, they were thinking about the same thing, or rather, I should say, about the same person — Corinne; thinking, however, each in a different way.

Bebe thought only of what a lovable little girl her new friend promised to be, and planned to visit her just as soon as she could. Charley was thinking of what seemed to him the very forlorn condition of Auntie Stone's protégé — the child of poverty, and a drunken father; and his heart smote him sorely for the unkind words he had uttered that day, and he would have been very glad if he could have recalled them. He resolved that he would be very, very careful not to speak unkind words about people in the future; and, "Oh!" thought he, "what if my sister were in her place, and somebody should talk about her so!"

Just here the reveries of both, pleasant and unpleasant, were broken in upon by Aunt Patty's call to dinner, after which Bessie, driven by Bob, the boy who had charge of her, took the children back to Sunday-school, where Bebe hoped she would meet Corinne again. But she was not there.

CHAPTER XVII
Charley's Tramp

One morning after breakfast, Mr. Reade remarked that he thought of going over to Sweetbrier Farm to see Mr. Stone on some business, and he told Bebe that if she wished, she might go with him.

Charley had declared his intention to go fishing, so his sister, who was generally very lonely when he was away for any length of time, was glad that she would not have to stay at home alone.

Bebe was soon ready, and so was old Bessie. It was a beautiful morning, and they had a delightful drive to Sweetbrier Farm, and a cordial welcome from "Auntie Stone," while Corinne smiled her pleasure.

"Nathan's in the potato patch," Mrs. Stone said, in answer to Mr. Reade's inquiry, as to where he should find her husband; so leaving Bebe to have a good time with Corinne, he went in search of him. "Auntie Stone" sent the two girls off to "have a good romp together," which they were not at all unwilling to do.

Although Corinne had been at the farm but a short time, she felt entirely at home and perfectly happy; and nothing could have pleased good Mrs. Stone more than the sight of the children running, hopping, skipping, and jumping over the grass and among the trees.

After running and playing until they were tired, the girls sat down under an old apple tree in the orchard, to rest and talk.

"Why haven't you been to Sunday-school?" asked Bebe, plucking a clover leaf, and sticking it between her teeth.

"I'd like to come, well enough; but I don't know anybody there."

"Oh, that's nothing; besides, I'm sure you know me," said Bebe, "and you could come into our class. We've a splendid teacher; her name is Mrs. Andrews; she makes the lessons so pleasant; explains everything so nicely, you know, and talks, and sometimes tells stories to make us understand the lesson better. Oh, you'd like her ever so much! Come next Sunday, won't you?"

"Yes," said Corinne, "I will if Aunt Anna is willing."

"Oh, she'll be willing," Bebe asserted, confidently. "I'll ask her before I go. She'll be glad to have you, I'm sure."

After a little more talk about the school, Bebe asked, softly: "Corinne, are you a Christian?"

"Yes," answered Corinne, with a happy light in her eyes; "are you?"

Bebe nodded her head affirmatively. "I'm glad, ain't you?" she asked.

"Yes, indeed," said Corinne. "I don't know what or where I'd be to day if I wasn't."

"Oh, but come now," exclaimed Bebe, "here we are sitting talking, and presently papa will be going home." And the lively little girl sprang up from her seat, and, followed by Corinne, raced away to the barn, to climb into the loft and tumble about in the hay; throwing aside with the light-hearted forgetfulness of childhood all sober thoughts for a time being. They had a gay time together, and a nice lunch of pie and milk under the trees, and then it was time for them to part. Mr. Reade, having talked farm and church business with Mr. Stone to his heart's content, was now quite ready to go. So with a "tight hug and hard kiss,"—as Bebe expressed it,—the girls separated, and old Bessie jogged off at her own leisurely, not-to-be-hurried pace; and thus ended one of the many happy days spent by Corinne and Bebe together.

About the middle of August, Charley had returned one afternoon from another of his fishing expeditions, and came running to find Bebe, greeting her with, "Say, Bebe, what do you 'spose I brought home with me to-day?"

"Why, I guess you caught a frog, a minnow, or maybe a tadpole," answered Bebe, mischievously.

"No I didn't, Bebe Reade. I caught a fine string of fish."

"You mean a string of fine fish, don't you, Master Charles?"

"Oh, my! you *are* smart; but if you don't want to hear what I was going to tell you, it's all right." And Charley walked off with his head up, and a "high and mighty" air, but inwardly much disappointed, because he had not told his news.

"Now, Charley, don't get stiff so quickly; I'm sorry I teased you," called Bebe, running after and catching him by the arm. "I was only in fun. Tell me what you were going to."

"Well, if you behave yourself, I will," replied Charley, too eager to tell to even feign anger long. "Bebe, I brought home a tramp!"

"Oh, Charley Reade! A tramp? A 'really and truly' tramp?" cried Bebe, coming to a halt, and looking about her distrustfully.

"Yes, a 'really and truly' tramp," repeated Charley, enjoying his sister's dismay; "only it's a boy tramp, and a jolly fellow he is too."

"Where is he?" asked Bebe.

"In the kitchen, getting something to eat. He's to stay all night, if papa's willing. I'm going now to tell him all about it." And off he ran.

Bebe went toward the house, and around to the kitchen, where she found the wonderful "tramp" sitting at the table, eating some bread and meat.

The boy was rather rough-looking, but appeared to be good-natured; and his clothing, though coarse and plain, was whole and clean. He was by no means what Bebe considered a "a really and truly tramp." Her ideal was a far more ferocious, tattered, grimy individual than the boy before her, who, having finished his meal, arose, and thanking Aunt Patty, signified his willingness to go to work. The work was to saw a pile of wood that had been brought that morning. Bebe eyed the stranger rather suspiciously, as he passed her on his way to the woodpile.

When he reached it, he pulled off his jacket and went to work with a will, that showed that, tramp though he might be, he was not averse to sawing wood. Presently, Bebe cautiously approached, and sat down on a log near by, and watched him as he laid the sticks upon the woodhorse, and with a steady hand sent the bright saw through them. After a while, the little girl grew tired of sitting there in silence, so she summoned sufficient courage to ask the boy his name.

"My name is Clarence Burton," he answered, pausing a moment to wipe the perspiration from his forehead.

"Clarence," repeated Bebe slowly, as if turning over in her mind whether or not this was a suitable name for a tramp.

"Yes," said the boy, "the name is all right, if the owner isn't."

Beginning to lose some of her awe of the "tramp," Bebe ventured next to inquire if he had lost his way, and where he lived.

No, hadn't exactly lost his way, he told her; as to where he lived, he didn't live anywhere just now.

"Haven't you any home at all?" exclaimed Bebe, pityingly.

The boy shook his head, and again answered, "No." But we need to glance back for a moment, and see how our friend Clarence came from his comfortable home with Mother Carter, to the condition in which we now find him.

When Clarence reached home that evening, after having concluded his errand, he found the little shop quite dark, which he thought strange, for Mother Carter was accustomed to light up early, especially on rainy evenings. Cautiously feeling his way, avoiding the open trap-door as he went by, he found the lamp and lighted it. He first went into the little room at the back of the shop: there was no one there. Coming back, he directed the rays of the lamp into the cellar. There he saw his old friend lying on the floor unconscious. Quickly descending the steps, he laid his hand upon her head, fearing she was dead. His touch seemed to arouse her, for she gave a faint sigh, and then a feeble groan. Finding that she had only fainted, he hastened up the cellar steps and out into the street, running in his haste against a policeman who was passing.

"What's the matter with you, boy?" growled the officer; "where are you running?"

Clarence excused himself, and explained what had happened, and the policeman returned with him to the shop. They carried Mother Carter from her uncomfortable and painful position, and placed her upon her bed.

The boy called in a neighbor, and then hurried away in search of a doctor. Having succeeded in finding one, he hurried back to the side of his injured friend, the doctor promising to follow in a short time. He came, examined the sufferer, prescribed and went away, saying that he would call in the morning.

The injured woman passed a very restless night, and seemed to suffer greatly. Clarence watched by her faithfully all night, the neighbor having returned to her home.

When the doctor came in the morning, he examined the patient again, more carefully than he had done the evening before. He found that she was more seriously hurt than he had at first thought, having received internal injuries, besides having hurt her back and head by striking it against the cellar steps. All this, added to a not over-robust frame, and her advanced age, worked against her, and the doctor told Clarence that he feared the good old woman's days were numbered.

The boy was filled with sorrow at this intelligence, and at the prospect of again losing a friend. He watched by her bedside continually, leaving her only when relieved by the kind neighbor, who came in as often as she could, or to attend to the little shop.

One morning Mother Carter called him to her, and asked him to tell her what the doctor had said about her condition, and, seeing him hesitate, she said: "Go on, my boy, I don't mind hearing; I feel that my time has come, and I'm perfectly willing to go. Don't the doctor think I'll go soon?"

Clarence could not answer in words, so he simply nodded his head, while the tears dropped from his eyes and fell on the withered hand stretched out to him.

"Don't cry, my boy," said Mother Carter again. "I'm just a bit sorry to leave you; but, lad, trust in God; he'll make a way for you, and raise up friends to take the place of the ones he calls away."

Once again did she comfort him, and then directed him to see that she was buried decently, and to have her little business stock and household belongings sold, and pay her funeral expenses, together with her few debts, with the money; if anything was left after he had done this, he was to keep it for himself.

How glad Clarence was in the midst of his sorrow, that he was there to perform these little acts for the lonely old woman, who looked on him quite as a son! He felt that he could in this way repay her for the kindness she had shown him in receiving him into her home when the finger of suspicion was pointed at him. He felt that he *never could* repay her for leading his wayward feet into the straight and narrow way; but it was a comfort to feel that he could do something.

During her illness, Mother Carter received many little attentions from the neighbors, to whom she had always been a friend, and with whom she had never had a difficulty.

Peacefully and quietly did the spirit of the dear old woman pass away, and once more Clarence found himself alone. He carried out the last wishes of his kind friend as faithfully as he could, and when all was done, and the little shop closed up, he went out again into the streets. He had a little money in his pockets, part of which was the remainder of his own savings.

"What shall I do now?" he asked himself; "and where shall I go?" he wondered, as he slowly walked along the sunny thoroughfares. "I'm so tired of the city, I've a mind to go to the country somewhere, and get work there, if I can."

Pleased at the thought, he made his way to the depot, and finding that he had enough money to carry him to Brierton, he purchased a ticket to that place, being attracted by the name, and in a few minutes was leaving the city far behind.

CHAPTER XVIII

The Reunion

"Brierton! Brierton!" was at length called, as the train rolled up to the little station; and Clarence was soon standing upon the very spot where, but a short time before, his sister Corinne had stood.

Unlike her, he had no home in view. He struck out for the wood which was close by, and whose cool shade offered him at least a place to think what next to do.

He really enjoyed rambling along under the trees; it had been so long since he had been in the country. Coming to a brook, he followed its course for a while, partly to see where it would lead him, and partly because it furnished him something to divert his mind from its perplexities.

Suddenly he was startled to hear a voice call "Halloo!" and, looking up, his eyes fell upon our friend, Charley Reade, who was perched upon a rock by the brook, rod in hand, waiting for the fish to bite.

"Halloo!" answered Clarence, sitting down beside him. "Having good luck?"

"Not yet," was the reply. "I haven't caught a single fish. But there! Be quiet. I believe I've got one!"

Sure enough he had. And when the line was pulled in, it brought with it a fine trout.

The day proved to be a good one for fishing. Charley was delighted; for soon there lay a goodly number of flapping, panting victims at his feet.

Having fished until he was satisfied, he turned his attention to his companion, whom he catechised pretty freely. "Well, I don't know," he said, reflexively, in answer to the query whether he knew where

Clarence could find work; "My aunt might give you something to do. Anyway, we can go and see, and you can get something to eat. Hungry?"

"Guess I am," answered Clarence. "You'd be hungry too, if you hadn't had anything to eat since early this morning."

And so the two boys started off together in the direction of Charley's home.

They found Aunt Patty willing to give the wanderer some food, for which he was to pay afterward by sawing wood. As to whether he might remain all night, was left for Mr. Reade to decide; and Charley, as we know, was gone in quest of his father, in order to learn his decision.

"Clarence," said Bebe, after a short silence, "have you a father and mother?"

"My mother is dead," said he, evasively.

"Have you any sisters or brothers?" persisted Bebe.

"I've a sister," said the boy, in a tone that plainly said he wished she would not ask him any more questions. But Bebe was too intent on making herself acquainted with the past history of the "tramp" to heed his tone.

"Where is your sister?" she demanded.

"I don't know," said Clarence, sawing away desperately, hoping by this means to put an end to the dialogue.

It was interrupted in another way, however; for just then Charley made his appearance upon the scene. And throwing himself down upon the ground, he began to pick up handfuls of chips and throw them vigorously, this way and that.

"What are you doing, Charley Reade?" cried Bebe, as one of the handfuls flew over her. "I think you are very rude."

"Oh, I beg your pardon, Miss Reade," exclaimed the mischievous boy, springing to his feet and making a very low bow; "but really I couldn't help doing something to relieve my feelings."

"Well, please don't relieve your feelings on me, next time," said Bebe, severely. "But what are you so excited about?"

"Why, you see, I've got some good news for my tramp," said Charley, resuming his seat.

Clarence laughed. He did not object to being called a "tramp" one bit, at least by Charley.

"I asked papa," continued the boy, "if he wouldn't let Clarence stay here; but he said 'No, he didn't need another boy."

"Well," said Bebe, ruefully, "I don't call that good news."

"Oh, but you see you don't wait until I can finish."

"Because you are so provokingly long about telling," retorted his sister.

"And you are so provokingly impatient," returned Charley. But seeing that Bebe began to look a little ruffled, he pitched into the middle of his news, very much after the fashion in which he would have vaulted into a pile of hay.

"We're to take him to Auntie Stone's in the morning. Mr. Stone told papa that he wanted a boy to help about the place."

"But maybe he won't take Clarence; what then?" suggested Bebe. The boy, with his honest face, had thoroughly enlisted her sympathy, and she was as much interested in seeing him provided for as if he had been a relative.

"Oh, I'm pretty sure he'll take him," answered Charley, confidently. "Papa says he is too, especially as I recommend him." And Charley walked off whistling, while Bebe, in obedience to a call from Aunt Patty, went into the house.

Clarence finished the wood by nightfall, had his supper, and was given a bed in the attic. The next morning, after breakfast, Charley, Clarence, and Bebe started off together for Sweetbrier Farm.

It was a long walk. But they did not mind this, since they could take their time, and rest as often as they pleased.

When they reached the house, they saw Corinne sitting on the doorstep, paring apples. At least, this had been her occupation; but she had stopped, and was now bending over a torn newspaper. So interested was she in what it contained, that she did not notice the young people.

"Heigho, what's the news?" called the irrepressible Charley. "Anything strange?" The sound of his voice startled the little girl; but when her eyes fell upon the three visitors she sprang up, scattering the contents of her lap in every direction, and, rushing toward Clarence, threw her arms about his neck, passionately exclaiming, "Oh, Clarence!"

"If it isn't my own dear little sister!" cried he, returning her embrace with a will. For a while they all acted as though they had lost their wits. Charley hopped about on one leg; Corinne cried, and so did Bebe, for company; while Clarence did not know whether to laugh or cry. He felt like doing both at once; but compromised the matter by doing a little of each in turn.

In the midst of the confusion "Auntie Stone" came upon the scene; and seeing her little adopted daughter clinging to a strange lad, and noting the general excitement, demanded, in perplexed tones, the cause of it all. She also asked: "Who is that you have there, Corrie?"

"Oh, Aunt Anna, it's Clarence, my brother, whom I thought I would never see again!"

"Well! well! well! Who'd have thought it? How did it all come about?" And Auntie Stone looked inquiringly at Bebe, who said: "Tell her about it, Charley."

Nothing loth, in graphic style Master Charley told the whole story, beginning from where he met his "tramp" by the brook. During his recital, one more listener was added to the group, in the person of Mr. Stone. When Charley was through, he turned to Clarence and asked him if what he had heard was true — if he really had come to Brierton to get work.

"Yes, sir, it's so," answered the boy.

"And where have you been all this time, that your sister has not heard from you?" asked Mr. Stone, looking at him a little suspiciously.

Then Clarence told the tale of his wanderings, haps and mishaps; and his hearers were both interested and moved.

Auntie Stone could say nothing but "Well! well! well!" and wipe her glasses on the corner of her apron.

"Just see how God works! His hand is in all this," said Mr. Stone, gravely.

"Yes, indeed," said his wife, beginning to regain her composure.

"Anna," continued the good man, "I believe that God means that we shall rear these two children; else why should they be led right here to our door so miraculously?"

"Why, indeed?" said Auntie Stone.

"Well, what do you say, Anna?"

"I say what you say, Nathan."

"Then I say they shall both stay with us, and be to us as our own flesh and blood."

"I say so too," rejoined his wife, delightedly. It was just what she wished; but not knowing how her husband would regard the idea, she had said nothing about it.

"Now, Clarence," said Mr. Stone, turning to our young friend, who was so astonished that he could scarcely speak, "now, Clarence, what have you to say to staying here with us?"

"Say!" exclaimed Clarence, his voice trembling with emotion; "I don't know how to thank you enough; but I give you my word that I will prove my gratitude to you, by faithfully serving you in every way I can."

"All right, my boy, all right; I believe you will." And Mr. Stone left the group.

Auntie Stone, too, knowing that the long separated brother and sister would like to be alone for a while, called Charley and Bebe to come with her and see old Polly, the cat, and her new family of six kittens.

When Clarence and Corinne were left to themselves, such a talk as they had!

Corinne told all about her long illness and her kind friends and their care. "And, oh, Clarence," she cried, as her eyes fell upon the old newspaper which had fallen from her hand when she saw her brother, "see!" And she pointed to a certain paragraph. This was what Clarence read:

"Yesterday, about ten o'clock, A.M., a man, while crossing K — — — Street, was knocked down and run over by a runaway horse and wagon. He was fatally injured, and was carried to the hospital, where he died after suffering a great deal. Before he died, the man told a sad story of a debauched life. He stated that his name was James Burton, and that he had two children, a boy and a girl, whom he had deserted at the death of their mother, because he did not wish to be burdened with them. He expressed sorrow for his misspent life, but laid all the blame on whisky."

The name of the paper and its date were torn off; but Clarence and Corinne had no doubt that the poor unfortunate was none other than their father. And their hearts softened as they thought of his sad end.

But their quiet was now at an end. For Charley and Bebe came running toward them, exclaiming: "Why, what a time you have been talking! Here it's time for us to go home!"

Auntie Stone insisted on giving them all a lunch before they separated; and then the children took leave of each other, and Charley and Bebe set out for home alone.

Mr. Reade and Aunt Patty were delighted when they heard the result of the visit to Sweetbrier Farm.

In time, Clarence and Corinne were considered a part of Brierton. They attended the same school that Charley and Bebe attended, and were regularly at Sunday-school, the two girls being in the same class.

Charley and Clarence were inseparable companions; and the steady, manly course of the latter exerted such a good influence upon the impetuous Charley, that Mr. Reade determined that the two boys should be educated together. So when the time came for Charley to leave home and the Brierton school, he persuaded Mr. Stone to let Clarence go too. The boy had endeared himself to both Mr. Stone and his wife, and had rendered himself a necessity to Sweetbrier Farm — so much so that they were loth to let him leave them, even for a time. But "Uncle Nathan" was sure that there was "something in that boy that ought to be brought out," and so it was settled that he should go. Corinne and Bebe too were so much attached to each other, that Auntie Stone said it would be a pity to separate them. So they were sent away together to boarding school.

CHAPTER XIX
Conclusion

Years have passed since the events last chronicled in my narrative. And now, we go again to the same spot which we saw at the beginning of our story.

The old cottage has disappeared; and in its place stands a tasteful house, with a pretty garden in front. Inside, sitting by a table, reading, is a tall, pleasant-faced young man. Near him is a young woman, sewing. Though they have greatly changed, we can recognize in the grave, open face of the young man our old friend Clarence, and in the gentle, refined face of the young woman our little Corinne.

Liberally educated by their beloved foster parents, Mr. and Mrs. Stone, they had returned to the old country home, where Corinne devoted herself to the dear friends, who were both in failing health, partly brought about by worry and anxiety occasioned by reverses, which left them, in a measure, dependent upon their foster children. And Corinne was glad that now she could prove her affection and gratitude to "Uncle Nathan" and "Aunt Anna" by lovingly and faithfully ministering to them.

She secured a position as teacher in the Brierton school; while Clarence, who had shown no special taste for being a "doctor's boy," had, contrary even to his own expectations, developed a strong desire to be a doctor. He had therefore studied medicine, and now proceeded to build up a practice in the home of his early days. He was fortunately enabled to succeed, even beyond his fondest hopes.

One day he went to look at the old home, but found it and an adjoining old house gone, and the pretty dwelling noticed at the commencement of this chapter built where they stood.

The house was just finished, and was for rent. He was seized with a desire to live in it. Accordingly, he rented and furnished the house, letting it in turn to a family in which he boarded. He had a good practice, and sent home regularly to Brierton every penny he could spare.

Thus, by the exertions of their two adopted children, the feeble couple lived in peace and comfort, enjoying the fruits of their labors. Truly, the bread they had "cast upon the waters" had, after many days, returned.

They dearly loved the tall, broad-shouldered young doctor, who took advantage of every opportunity to spend a few days with them; but they considered Corinne their "sunbeam." And this she really was. No trouble, no care, was thought by the gentle girl too much to bestow upon those who had done so much for her and her dear brother.

Changes, too, the years have brought to the Reade household. Mr. Reade is still pastor of the little church at Brierton. Aunt Patty, long since passed away; and Bebe, now a demure little woman, is housekeeper for her father, who, in the fondness of his heart, thinks that never had another man a daughter such as his. Charley is in business in L— — —, the scene of the trials of his old friend Clarence.

Mr. Emory, long before, had found out, through the confession of Sam Baker, that Clarence was innocent of the deed of which he had believed him guilty; but he could find no trace of the boy to tell him so. He finally had that opportunity, however, but not until his former clerk was Dr. Burton. The good man was delighted to know of his success, but regretted deeply the injustice he had done him in accusing him of taking the money.

There is sorrow as well as joy in our closing chapter. The time came when Clarence and Corinne must bid a long farewell to their kind benefactors—sorrow to the brother and sister, but peace and joy to the dear old couple, who followed each other within a short space of time to the grave.

Then Clarence took his sister to the home that was waiting for her; and so the promise of his early days was fulfilled.

The brother and sister were very happy in this little home of theirs; and Corinne was quite proud of the plate upon the door, bearing the name of Dr. Clarence Burton.

They had not seen their friends, the Grays, since they left N— — —, but they had heard from them occasionally. Mary Gray was dead. She did not live long after their removal. Helen was married to a nephew of good Dr. Barrett.

Miss Rachel Penrose was still living, but was a confirmed invalid; and although unwilling to do so, was obliged to employ some one to take care of her.

Corinne called one day to see Miss Rachel, thinking that perhaps she regretted the many hardships and weary days she had caused her to endure; but she found her the same as ever—stingy and hard.

Questions she asked, and plenty of them; but no word of regret did she utter for past injustice, or of pleasure at the different and improved condition of her former little maid. When Corinne asked if she should read a chapter in the Bible, she gave a cold and indifferent assent; and the only comment she made, when the reading was done, was to say it was "mighty queer how things turned out well for some folks, and ill for others"; which remark showed that she had paid but little attention to the blessed words Corinne had been reading: "Let not your heart be troubled," etc.

Sadly Corinne took her departure, giving a sigh of relief when once more out in the open air, away from the close and depressing atmosphere of the house that had once been her home.

Once or twice after this she went to see Miss Rachel, each time reading to her from the "Book of books," regardless of the many sarcastic remarks she saw fit to make, and the apparent indifference with which she listened to the reading; and never was any one more surprised than was Corinne, when, after the death of Miss Rachel, it was found that she had remembered her generously in her will.

How much good she had done her former guardian by her visits, Corinne did not know. But she did know that she had "done what she could."

The addition to the modest possessions of the brother and sister allowed them to expand a little. Corinne insisted first on fitting up a nice office for her brother; and then she indulged in the luxury of a girl, to help with the housework. This girl was the one who had watched by the bedside of Miss Rachel Penrose during her last hours, and who loved the bright face of the only person who had cared enough about the once busy seamstress to come and see her, when she was no longer able to work.

"God's ways are not our ways," repeated Corinne, softly, as she and Clarence walked slowly home from church one bright Sunday. The words she quoted had been the substance of the sermon to which they had listened that morning.

"That they are not, Corrie," rejoined her brother, "and I'm glad of it; for I'm afraid that our ways would often lead us into doubtful places. Corrie,"—he continued as he paused before a house on a wide, tree-shaded street,—"Corrie, do you remember going with me, one afternoon, to gather chips for our poor mother?"

"Remember? I guess I do," was the answer; "for it was then we met our dear Miss Helen."

"Well, this is the very house that was then being built, and where we got those chips."

"Well?" said Corinne, inquiringly.

"Well," answered Clarence, "I've bought this house."

"Why, Clarence! It's too large for us to live in—just us two."

"I guess not," said Clarence, with a twinkle in his eye. "Wait and see."

Well, she did wait, and wondered very much at the way in which Clarence went to work and furnished that house. But she had great faith in her brother and whatever he did; so she concluded that it was all right. They moved out of the old home into the new, and then Clarence went away; and when he returned, brought with him Mr. Reade, Bebe, and Charley.

The sequel could be read without the book. But there was a marriage speedily, and the bride was Bebe Reade, while the groom was Dr. Burton. There was another, also, soon after. This time Corinne Burton and Charley Reade took the principal parts. Then did Corinne agree that the new house was not a bit too large.

Mr. Reade took up his abode with his son and daughter; and so the old homestead at Brierton was deserted, and the good minister preached to a new people.

And so we take leave of our friends, having followed them through both good and ill. "God's ways are not our ways." Let this be remembered by all disheartened ones. Into every shadow let his presence shine, and above every storm let his voice be heard.

> "Blind unbelief is sure to err,
> And scan his work in vain.
> God is his own interpreter,
> And he will make it plain."

The End.

The Album of a Heart

R. Nathaniel Dett

Introduction.

It has been our very great pleasure to be associated with the author of this little volume, as teachers in Lane College, now for three years.

He has convinced us that he is a musician of the first water and a poet of no mean gifts. That he is a close student and that nature has whispered into his ears many of her secrets, those who read the beautiful poems contained herein will not doubt. Young people, and old people as well, can not spend a passing hour more pleasantly and profitably than in reading literature teeming with thoughts that are pure, sentiments that are noble, and ideals that are high. Believing this little volume replete with the elements named above, we most heartily commend its careful perusal to all who read and appreciate.

Trusting that on its mission of comfort and cheer, it may find a place in many houses and a nook in many hearts,

We are very respectfully,

GEO. F. PORTER,

FRANK H. RODGERS.

Jackson, Tennessee.

Foreword.

The heart is a gallery in which many pictures indeed are hung; and there are grave ones or gay ones or both, according as has been the experience; vivid or faint are they according to the circumstances which caused them to be; and the framing (not the least of the picture) is deeply precious or indifferently so, according to the tenderness of regard in which the picture itself is held.

How often when the mind is free from outside cares will it indulge itself in tender musings over things which are in the main the works of its own creating; and even over those scenes which are less lovely will it oftimes linger, held by that strange fascination which inevitably binds creator to the thing created.

Perhaps every heart may not boast a gallery, but each will have its own little album,—an album of miniatures perhaps, but because miniatures none the less true.

Who is it that idly looking over a collection of portraits or sketches has not been suddenly arrested by the familiarity of some unknown face or scene? Even so, dear reader, if in an idle moment while glancing through these pages you are struck by the seeming familiarity of what is portrayed, be not surprised; it is only that one of these little sketches has a counterpart among those pictures garnered for your own heart's album.

R. NATHANIEL DETT.
Lane College,
Wednesday, May 24, 1911.

The Traumerei.

To Olga.

Night fell at last, as night is wont to fall,
Gathering darkness from the muted wind.
And like the leaves that in the Autumn fall
So quietly to earth, the shadows downwards
Slow at first, then faster silent fell.
Nightly born anew the infant stars,
Children of the shadows, childlike came
To timidly peep forth with curious gaze.
All was silent, till a tactful bird
Conscious of the moment opportune,
Rais'd an even song whose rapturous note
Made the previous quietude seem strange.

I entranced lay. On tip-toe, Sleep,
Jealous mistress of the evening hours,
Came and touch'd my eyelids with her hand;
And, departing for her nightly rounds,
Left Dreams, her sister, guardian in her stead.

Dreams was not slow to ply her magic art.
To a mountain's top whose gorgeous slopes
A Pizgah in an Eden might have made,
Thither she bore me. There to my 'stonished view
Expos'd a scene, the strange phantasmagoria
Of whose fabric only could be spun
By the magic of that witch-maid, Dreams.

As in a mirror, one his vision sees,
Self viewing self,—so I the vision saw.
Three glorious angels floated me in air—
And yet not me, but just those parts of me

Members most representative in all the ways
And moods and walks of life's activity.

One bore my head, another bore my hands
While still another bore my very heart.
I saw, and seeing understood. All three
Each for herself desir'd but the control
Of me, the man—my seraph-guarded members
I knew but emblems were of means of sway.

On high the first one raised up my head,
Vast empires still unconquer'd were reveal'd.
By intuition swift I sudden knew
'Twas with me, but to make those empires mine.

Ambition fir'd me. Breathes anywhere a soul
Wherein doth dwell no love of regal sway?
Me, King of Earth, no vassalage in heaven
Could ever woo. 'Twas done. I had decided
Then and there: but in the uplifted gaze
Of the two others I read the mandate: "Wait."

The second laid my hands upon a Harp;
And at my touch, straightway from the strings
Wondrous, mcllifluous harmonies unknown to men
With strange accord pour'd forth their dulcet strains.

Oh Music,—of the holy arts most high!
Shall these poor hands thy subtle power employ.
Thy holy essence may I understand,
Till feeling these the very stones and trees
Acknowledge me their master! Once again
I would have made decision—but a sense
Of something yet to come appr'ended me.

Now that Fair She who bore my own full heart
Did but press it closer to her own
As loth to leave it; drooping low her head
In deep affection touch'd it with her lips.
Quiet-like then began she a song
Wild, yet soft, free and yet so pure
The melody, its sweetness made it sad.
Thrill'd by its tremor past all I could endure
Trembling to the point of tears—I woke.

Kingdoms, Power, Endless Wealth—not these!
Mastery, Art, Ceaseless Fame—not these!
But dear Heart-Angel, visit thou my dreams.
Thou only come, I yield to thy control!

And when 'tis mine to take that last long sleep,
Grant me to wake but in a world with thee!
There let the tremor of thy love-born song
Waft me on to Rapture's highest plane;
Until no longer able to endure
I lose myself in God's Eternity.

That's So!

There'd be no Pleasure were there no Pain;
E 'en Sunshine would pall were there no Rain:
We could not smile, if in all the years
We'd never shed a few sad tears.
What need of ambition if all were gain?
There'd be no Pleasure were there no Pain.

At Niagara.

No, No! Not tonight, my Friend,
I may not, cannot go with you tonight.
And think not that I love you any less
Because this now I'd rather be alone.
My heart is strangely heavy; unwonted thoughts
Have so infused themselves into my mind
That altogether there is wrought in me
A sort of hapless mood, whose phantom power
Born perhaps of my own fantasies
Has ta'en me. By its subtle spell
I'm wooed and changed from what's my natural self.
I am so possessed I can but wish
For nothing else save this and solitude.
If in companionship I sought relief
Yours indeed would be the first I'd seek.
There is none other whom I so esteem,
None who quite so perfect understands.
Your presence always is a soothing balm,
Ne'er failing me when troubled. But tonight,
Forgive me, Friend—I'd rather be alone.
Leave me, let me with myself commune.
Presently if no change come, I shall go
Stand in the shadowed gorge, or where the moon
Throws her silver on the rippling stream,

List to the sounding cat'ract's thundering fall
Or hark to spirit voices in the wind.
For methinks sometimes that these strange moods
Are Heaven-sent us by the jealous God
Who'd thus remind us that no human love
Can fully satisfy the longing heart.
Perhaps an intimation sent to souls
That he would speak somewhat, or nearer draw.
Therefore I'll to Him. Talking waters, stars,
The moon and whisp'ring trees shall make me wise
In what it is He'd have my spirit know.
And Nature singing from the earth and sky
Shall fill me with such peace, that in the morn
I'll be the gay glad self you've always known.
Urge me no further, now that you understand.
A nobler friend than you none ever knew—
But not this time. Tonight I'll be alone;
And if from moonlit valley God should speak
Or in the tumbling waters sound a call
Or whisper in the sighing of the wind,
He'll find me with an undivided heart
Patient waiting to hear; but Friend,—alone.

I Stood by the Caves of Memory.

To Prof. P. D. Sherman, Oberlin College.

I stood by the Caves of Memory;
Suddenly taken unawares
I felt myself o'erpowered by some strange force
Which flung itself upon me and fiercely strove
To drag me down, whither I knew not.
Helpless in my distress I called on God—
Straightway the thing fled from me
And I saw it go running black and naked
To hide itself among the caverned recesses.
Once there it turned and hotly fixed its eyes upon me—
And I recognized it. 'Twas the thought
Of an evil deed, done in those past days
When Passion was master of my spirit.

Misercordia.

Where, in the forest stands a loom
    Of shadows, there stood I;
Methought from somewhere in the gloom
    I heard an owlet cry.

So weird the scream, a lurid gleam
    Of light sped with the tone;
But in my heart I felt no start,
    The voice seemed like my own.

For sure no owl 'mid shadows foul
    Could voice such fearful cry;
No heart could know such awful woe—
    No, none could save I.

That rantipole was my own soul
    In mis'ry shunning light;
O'ercome with grief, to find relief,
    Had shrieked out in the night!

The Mountain

To my pupil, Mr. O. B. Payne, Lane College, 1911.

I love the mountain!
Tho' he frown on me
A kindness lurks beneath, that majesty;
A message writ those furrowed brows along
Forever says: "Be strong! Be strong!"

I love the mountain!
Tho' his lofty peak
Wind swept, cloud swept, towers lone and bleak,
No matter to what heights I would aspire,
Ever silent calls to me: "Climb higher!"

I love the mountain!
For its rocks and trees
Forever speak a thousand mysteries;
On that rugged brow, the humble sod
Lowly speaks not of itself but God.

I love the mountain!
Tho' he silent stand
His voice is stronger than a mighty band
Of clarion angels, loudly who proclaim
A loftier purpose and a nobler aim;
And so I love him all the more since he
Through noblest speech betrays his love for me.

Ditty.

A Butterfly paused on a Rose
　　And oh, so gently he pressed her;
Her tears of joy fell soft as the dew,
　　As he so gently caressed her.

Ah me! Ah me! Ah me!
　　Estranged forever from pleasure
Is the heart that in innocence yields
　　Its depths to fickle love's measure.

Did the Butterfly love the dear Rose
　　(Her heart was broken they say),
She was for him but a moment's delight
　　And then he flitted away.

Ah me! Ah me! Ah me!
　　Estranged forever from pleasure
Is the heart that in innocence yields
　　Its depths to fickle love's measure.

Be warned by the fate of the Rose
　　So soon and so sadly forsaken;
In soft-sounding word and gentle caress
　　'Tis easy to be quite mistaken.

Ah me! Ah me! Ah me!
　　Estranged forever from pleasure
Is the heart that in innocence yields
　　Its depths to fickle love's measure.

Pappy.

When I was a pickaninny
Many years ago, I 'members how my mammy used ter call me.
Up the creakin' stairs she came,
'Bout time for first cock crow,
An' turnin' back de kiver she would say:

    "Open yo' eyes,
    "Litt'l niggah;
    "Open yo' eyes,
    "Litt'l niggah;
    "Open yo' eyes, open yo' eyes.
    "Litt'l niggah, de daylight's come;
    "Litt'l niggah, de daylight's come."

Happy days for pickaninny;
Soon dey pass away:
Mammy's gone; she wid the saints in glory.
Mem'ry makes de tears come risin'
Oft at break o' day;
I hears a dear sweet voice which seems ter say:

    "Open yo' eyes,
    "Litt'l niggah;
    "Open yo' eyes,
    "Litt'l niggah;
    "Open yo' eyes, open yo' eyes.
    "Litt'l niggah, de daylight's come;
    "Litt'l niggah, de daylight's come."

Bagatelle

Life's a Spindle;
Both ends dwindle.

The Rubinstein Staccato Etude.

To Prof. G. C. Hastings, Oberlin Conservatory.

Staccato! Staccato!
Leggier agitato!
    In and out does the melody twist—
Unique proposition
Is this composition.
    (Alas! for the player who hasn't the wrist!)
Now in the dominant
Theme ringing prominent,
    Bass still repeating its one monotone,
Double notes crying,
Up keyboard go flying,
    The change to the minor comes in like a groan.
Without a cessation
A chaste modulation
    Hastens adown to subdominant key,
Where melody mellow-like
Singing so 'cello-like
    Rising and falling in wild ecstacy.
Scarce is this finished
When chords all diminished
    Break loose in a patter that comes down like rain,
A pedal-point wonder
Rivaling thunder.
    Now all is mad agitation again.
Like laughter jolly
Begins the *finale*;
    Again does the 'cello its tones seem to lend
Diminuendo ad molto crescendo.
    Ah! Rubinstein only could make such an end!

A Romance Sonata

I. Andante Teneramente.

Day kissed the hills at parting,
Whispered to the trees,
Glanced into her mirror-lake
And with a smile,
Silent withdrew herself into the night.

Drawn forth by Nature's witcheries I came,
Came and stood alone upon the strand.
And there I met you, met you mid the gloom
And the sad, sad sound of the sea.
Ah! souls betrothed by Heaven's kind ordaining,
No spoken word need they, their love prefacing.
I met you; changed was night to day,
The wail of the sea, a song of glad surprise.
I gazed on Nature, she flung back my joy;
I gazed on you, and sudden strangely moved
Could not repress the tears that all unbid,
That all unbid, but from my heart upsprang.

Day kissed the hills at parting
And I but kissed your hand;
Day whispered to the trees
And I but your fair name.

Day glanced into her mirror-lake,
I looked but in your eyes;
You with a smile
Silent withdrew yourself into the night.

II. *Arietta.*

I dreamed of you at morn;
    I thought I saw you smile,—
I woke, and lo! the bright sunbeams
    Shone round me all the while!

I dreamed of you at eve;
    Your voice I seemed to hear,—
I woke, and lo! a nightingale
    Sang at my window near.

Where perfumed flowers whisper
    To soft winds sighing south,
I dreamed you kissed me; lo, a rose
    Had fallen on my mouth.

III. *Cadenza Inganno.*

At dawn? Well, I am not certain;
But I know 'twas betimes of the morning;
From half-dreams I sudden was conscious
Of waking, with nerves all a-tingle
Hoping to hear it repeated.
For soft on the air, like a bugle,
Fell the low, sweet call of a robin!

Instant with the note came a vision
Of smiling fields and blowing flower bells;
Of lace-draped trees all shadowy with Spring.
Again I felt the joyous touch
Of your warm hand in mine,
As together we wandered
Like children, 'mid the fields

In the rapturous bloom of the weather.
And Oh! so strong was the fancy,
Scarce knowing the spirit that moved me
I sprang up and flung wide the casement.

Alas! there was no robin!
(Too soon, for yet chill was the weather.)
But a mocking-bird, oh, recreant deceiver!
Yet I might have forgiven the trickster
Were it not that with cry changed to cat-call,
He sped away o'er the hill tops
And seemed to laugh on derision!

IV. Nocturne.

The Moon and I are friends now;
Our friendship began
On that fatal night
When you and I parted—
Parted to meet no more.
I've told her all that happened,
All that used to be,
All I hoped would be
When she heard of how you once had loved me
And I believed you true,
She smiled, oh such a radiant smile,
And all the golden stars danced.
But when I said that now,
Banished from the bounds of your affection
A lonely exile, I,
Wandering only in the light of her pale beams,
She turned—the old Moon turned—
I swear she turned
And with a shivering sigh
Hid her face behind a darksome cloud.

V. Recitative.

In vain! In vain!
All you do is vain!
Tho' you declare your love no longer lives,
And all your life be spent this one fact proving,
Yet 'tis all in vain,
For what I have is mine and mine shall be.
No word or deed-built avalanche can defame
Your perfect image 'stablished in my heart.
Mem'ries of hours we have spent together
Lie peaceful in my breast,
Deep-sea pearls unshaken by the storm.
To-day may change and the future bring
Such strife, confusion, inharmonious scenes
That viewed from now impossible would seem;
Yet there is no power in Earth or Heaven
Nor even from the raging depths of Hell
Can tear from me the mem'ries that I have,
Nor insidious dissipate the past!

VI. Largo Con Tristezza.

Drop, drop, my Tears,
And let your sodden sound
Only disturb this quiet solitude.
Drop, drop, my Tears,
Let this heavy heart
Surcease find, in your kind o'erflow.
Drop, drop, my Tears;
Drop, drop, my Tears.

Was it a voice ?
Comes someone?

Do forms appear
Most beloved, but which I would not see?
Only the trees that whispered,—
And I am alone.

Drop, drop, my Tears;
Rise ye full and free,
Float my grief upon your swelling tide.
Drop, drop, my Tears,
Let this heavy heart
Surcease find, in your kind o'erflow.
Drop, drop, my Tears;
Drop, drop, my Tears.

VII. Finale—Fuoco di Molto.

Rage ye Winds, rage with furious rage,
Resistless, relentless, sweep o'er land and sea,
Lash the wave, uproot the mighty oak,
Ruthless fling them hither, fling them yond!
Thus would I throttle the powers that be.

Burst ye mighty Tidal Wave, burst high,
Unloose ye wild White Horses of old Ocean,
Remorseless hurl into Eternity a nation!
Your rancor shall be play to that I'd use
Could I but lay my hand on Destiny.

And thou ,Vesuvius, in fierce eruption
As if from out the bowels of Hell, fling high
Your splatter in the very face of Heaven!
Your fury, oh how mild to that which burns
Within my breast 'gainst this that's come on me.

Why is it mine to suffer and why mine
To weep these tears of bitterness alone?
Mother of Destinies, fiercely I resent
The choice that makes me Sorrow's special child.
A thousand curses on the Fates, I say,
That robbed me of a scarcely tasted joy.

A thousand curses on the Fates, I say,
That robbed me of a love that once was mine;
On that which placed this seal upon my heart,
And drives me to a lasting hermitage.

Au Matin.

I watch'd the growing dawn that greyed my room;
Things visible rose ghostlike out of the gloom.
I watched again: It seemed a pearly ash had cover'd
    all;
Light and shade alike shar'd its finely sifted pall.
Hark! an awaken'd bird calls; greets the day with a
    glee:
But the morn brings me no gladness—I'm without thee!

Au Soir.

Moonlight Blue,
I and you
No sound heard,
Save a mocking bird
Who in delight
Enthralls the night.

But his bliss
Is naught to this
Which we know
Here below,
While on high
Floats wide his cry.

Starlight Sky,
You and I
Silence to each
Maketh speech.
Spoken proverb
Would but disturb,
Or canticle
Unloose the spell.

Unto the Moon
The bird, eftsoon,
"Will tell our bliss,—
Sufficient this.
Aught else would be
Unnecessary;
By touch of hand
We understand.

Now does joy
    Its bounds transcend,—
Would the night
    Might never end!
soft shine on us
    From above,
Beauteous Night
    Of perfect love.

Yield But Thy Love to Me

This poem was set to music by the author and sung by Miss Sarah Alexander at a Musical Round Table held by the author before the State Normal School session at Lane College, summer of 1909.

Yield but thy love to me
And I'll not ask to be
A king o'er empires great. Thy love
Were realm enough for me.

Yield by thy love to me
And I'll not fear to be
Wrapped cold in Death; Death in thy love
Were living joy to me.

Yield but thy love to me
And I'll not wish to be
In Paradise. Life in thy love
Were Heav'n itself to me.

Ode

To the Lane College Senior Class of 1911,
Messrs. J. Ashton Hayes, Oscar B. Payne, Thomas A. Bowers.

J. A. H.

There's a flower; 'tis the clover,
Known to every nature lover;
Honey-full its fragrant lips,
Where all day the work-bee sips;
Sweetest flower of the lea,
It has leaflets Three.

O. B. P.

Holy Writ from cover to cover
Read, O Heart, and there discover
What the abiding virtues be;
Let the Word admonish thee:—
Faith and Hope and Charity,
These the virtues Three.

T. A. B.

Draw aside high Heaven's curtain,
Dare to gaze within. I'm certain
Ruling there the Sacred Host,
Father, Son and Holy Ghost;
Tho' but one Sublimity,
God has Persons Three.

B. P. H.

Seniors, do you catch my meaning?
Surely now the Truth you're gleaning,
All of greatness that there be;
E'er concomitant with Three
Be yours. And may the Smile of Heaven
Bless this Class of Nineteen Eleven.

To the Sea.

To Dr. George W. Andrews, Oberlin Conservatory.
This poem was set to music by the author and sung by Miss Helen Mears,
contralto, Class of 1908, at the author's recital of original compositions,
Conservatory, Oberlin, June 9th, 1908.

All day long from my window
    I hear the sound of the sea;
The solemn sound of its deep profound
    Fathomless tranquility.
'Tis the song of its mighty spirit
    Whose inmost life is peace—
But from the pain of a love is vain
    The heart finds no release!

Twilight.

How still the twilight! the yet starless sky
Aweary leans upon the silent shore;
The day is dying and that solemn hush
Which Death alone commands pervadeth all things.
Deepens the gloom until my very soul
Attuned with Nature seems to sink and fade.
To sink and fade until I scarcely know
Whether 'tis I or Day that silent dies—
But no. It is not I that dying thus
In silence melts into a voiceless calm;
Tho' night's approaches bind all nature mute
Love knows no fetters. Free the soul proclaims
Its message—as the twilight sky sublime—
Oh deep as Death that folds the waning day,
Oh boundless as the mantle of its gloom,
Oh message that the very silence is telling
I love thee! I love thee! I love thee!

    See note to "Oh Whisp'ring Tree."

Berceuse.

To Baby Louise Kathryn Barnes.

Tears of angels that softly fall
Make the gentle rain;
They mourn for the flowers that soon must die
E'er they may come again:
So sleep my Baby, sleep my Baby,
Sleep and take your rest,
While angel woe for flowers flow
Sleep, Angel at mother's breast, oh sleep,
Sleep, Angel at mother's breast.

Harps of angels that softly sigh
Is the gentle wind,
Singing of the heavenly love
So great, eternal, kind;
So sleep my Baby, sleep my Baby,
Sleep and take your rest,
While angels paise in Aeolian lays
Sleep, Angel at mother's breast, oh sleep,
Sleep, Angel at mother's breast.

Eyes of angels that softly shine
Are the stars so bright
Peeping from the heavenly deeps
Softly say "Good Night";
So sleep my baby, sleep my baby,
Sleep and take your rest,
While angel eyes say "Good night" from the skies
Sleep, Angel at mother's breast, oh sleep,
Sleep, Angel at mother's breast.

Mistaken.

In jest you laid your head upon my heart
To hear it beat; and found a counterpart
Of your own heartbeats. Then you said in fun,—
"Surely we've two hearts that beat as one."
But maybe there's another reason too
(Of course it did not e'er occur to you);
I have no heart now, when we first did meet
You stole it. How then did you hear it beat?
No, what you heard as you lay on my breast
Were echoes mere, of your own heart's unrest.

After.

I stood on the mountain and called you;
And the birds, at my crying
Fled from their nests all affrighted.

I stood by the sea-shore and called you;
The broken waves, rolling inwards
But answered with meaningless sobbing.

Deep in the valley I called you;
Loudly, the wild errant echoes
Danced up the hillsides and mocked me.

Then spake the soul to the spirit,—
"Ne'er from the bird-haunted mountain
"Not from the echoing valley
"Nor where breaks the sob-hefted ocean,
"Shall she e'er answer your calling.
"Look in your heart if you'd find her—
"Who was the life of your loving;
"Look in your heart would you find her—
"Who was the joy of your living;
"There where mem'ry keeps vigil
"And grief is ever attendant
"Roams she again in the wild wood;
"Hearkens again to the ocean;
"Sings to the gossiping echoes.
"Tho' faded from earth as a blossom
"In the heart is forever enthroned."

Oh Whisp'ring Tree.

To Mrs. F. H. Goff, Glenville, Ohio.
This poem and "Twilight" were set to music by the author
and sung by one of the Conservatory vocal instructors,
Miss Florence Jenny, at the author's Recital of original compositions,
Oberlin Conservatory, June 9th, 1908.

Oh Whisp'ring Tree with arms outspread,
    Thy shape a heavenward pointer forms;
Still standing tho' an age hath fled
    Surviving still the storms.

Even so that soul whose roots are God
    Survives the storms of life like thee
Stands firm, tho' Fate rule with iron rod,—
    Oh Whisp'ring Tree.

A Melody that Haunts and Charms.

A melody that haunts and charms,
    Sweetly calling, sadly cheers.
A mem'ry reaching out gaunt arms
    To clutch but barren wasts of years.
Shapeless thoughts oppressive lower
    Thick as clouds which scourge the deep
When, lashed by the storm fiend's power
    Mighty oceans fall and leap—
Mystic half lights gleam and glimmer
    Mid the caverns of the soul;
Move with constant changing shimmer
    Fading always as they troll.
But the tides of Death, that ever
    'Round oblivion, cling and sob—
Only in their depths, may ever
    Pain of Heartbreak ease its throb.

Conjured.

Couldn't sleep last night!
    Just toss and pitch!
I'm conjured! I'm conjured!
    By that little witch!

My heart's all afire!
    My brain's got the itch!
I tell you I'm conjured
    By that little witch!

I'm "patchy" in feelings;
    It seems that a stitch
Has sewed me up inside out.
    Then there's a hitch

Whenever I try to think;
    Side track and switch
My thoughts do; and finally
    Dump me in the ditch.

And when I talk, my voice
    Seems all out of pitch;
When I think about her,
    My pulses, they twitch.

I'm in love or I'm crazy,
    I can't tell quite which;
But I know I've been conjured
    By that little witch!

Draw Nigh Unto Me.

Sweetheart, your hands are cold;
    Draw nigh unto me:
Shadows fall, the day grows old;
    Draw nigh unto me.
All day I've seen your downcast eye;
All day heard the troubled sigh
That would not stifle, though hard you try:
    Draw nigh unto me.

Come, lay your head upon my breast;
    Draw nigh unto me:
Love to freighted hearts brings rest;
    Draw nigh unto me.
Let me in your troubles share:
For you all grief I'd gladly bear;
Together we may laugh at care;
    Draw nigh unto me.

Sweetheart, in this world's a heart;
    Draw nigh unto me:
Undivided every part
    Beats for thee.
'Tis a heart o'erflown with love,
Sacred as the hearts that move
Round the throne of God. This heart
Is pleading now while near thou art.

You from its affection's tide
Naught but death shall e'er divide,
And twixt you and any ill
Gladly would itself instill;
This heart is mine. I offer thee
Its love,—unworthy tho' it be
Yet love constrains me, the love of thee;
Draw nigh unto me.

Faithfully Yours.

I had a corner in my heart,
    I kept it there for you;
It was the brightest, warmest spot
    That e'er a body knew.

When thoughts, like happy children came
    Along that way, I know
They always lingered round that spot,
    Charmed by its warmth and glow.

I have a corner in my heart,
    I keep it there for you;
It is as lonely sad a spot
    As e'er a body knew.

Time was a Thief: he stole the warmth,
    He stole the brightness too;
But 'till he steals my very self,
    I'll keep the spot for you.

Some day, perhaps, when you return,
    As wand'rers sometimes do,
We'll make old Time bring back the warmth,
    The glow and brightness too.

Then like true friends, we'll make amends,
    The covenant renew;
Once more the thrill of joy shall fill
    The spot I keep for you!

Elegy.

Note—Suella, eldest daughter of Rev. I. S. Person, pupil of
Prof. R. N. Dett died October 7th, 1910, at the early age of sixteen.
Her life was one of beauty, as all who knew her will readily testify.
She was distinguished by pronounced musical talent which promised
very great things—a promise, which owing to her premature death,
was only partially fulfilled.

She sleeps, our little Suella—
That blossom whom God pleased
To lend to earth for oh, so short a while
Now has drooped and died.
But though she died, a fragrance,
The fragrance of her presence
Lingers and always will linger with us still.
Even now it rises sweetly
From the swinging censors of our hearts.
She sleeps, our little Suella—
Peace, ye wailing winds,
Cease from your crying.
And, ye flowers of earth, with sorrow broken,
Be ye lift up. 'Tis season for rejoicing;
For hark the song of angels, ev'n as now,
She, starlike, is ushered in their midst.
And shall we,
Unworthy mortals, envy their thanksgiving?
Much 'tis rather
That glad we should be that we too, have known her—
Her, whom angels claim as one of them.
Moreover, we, inspired by her example,
Are resolved more perfectly to grow,
That when at last o'ercome with earth's travailing,
Face to face, and hand to hand,
Old friends united,

We may rise again to meet her in that land
Where there is no pain, no parting, disappointment,
    crying,
But one pure joy, fadeless and eternal,
Prescient, omnipotent, limitless, undying,
Reigns fore'er, sublime delight distilling.

Bishop Isaac Lane.

Note—Bishop Isaac Lane, founder of Lane College, Bishop for nearly forty years of the C. M. E. Church, celebrated his seventy-seventh birthday March 3rd, 1911; actively engaged in all the affairs of life.

Like some strong oak, the storm-fiend's blast defying,
So wrestling Time yet fails to throw him down;
Like some good ship, hard driv'n, safe comes to landing,
Him, likewise no seas of strife can drown.
Like Noah's dove that to the Ark returning
Brought to anxious hearts those signs of cheer,
So his word encouraging gives succor,
Uplifting fainting hearts dispelling fear.
O worthy Man! A nation pays thee homage,
A thankful race unites to call thee great;
Erudite, yet humble—of strength in meekness
Albeit of true goodness, thou a Potentate!

Lane College Song.

(Revised.)

Lane Collegians! Lane Collegians!
Lane Collegians, we—
O shout the song exultant,—
Wake the melody!
Lane, Lane, Lane,—
Loud let anthem ring!
With peans strong, the sound prolong,
While Lane of Thee we sing!

    Chorus.
Then hurrah for the Crimson,
Hurrah for the Blue—
Hurrah for the learning, that labors, too!
Then 'tis upward and onward,
Both faithful and true,
And the love that passeth knowledge, Lane,
We give to you!
And the love that passeth knowledge, Lane,
We give to you!
Hurrah, Lane! Hurrah, Lane! Hurrah, Lane!

On to victory! On to victory!
Yours to do or die:—
Now 'tis Lane men "Up, and at them"
Bravely with them vie:—
Hark the echo
Swells the jubilee
Of T-E- double N-E- double
S- double E!
    Chorus.

God before us, God that's o'er us,
Be Thou, God of Lane!
Guide us as we endeavor
Guard our feeble aim!
Lo! with splendor
Dawns the holy light
Of Truth we're free, and presently
We scale Parnassus' height.

    Chorus.

Remembrance.

To Mother.

Mother Dear, I'm not forgetting,
    In the soft dawn's pink and gray,
How you bade me rise me early
    For the travail of the day;
How you bade me rise me early,
    Bold and fearless face the Now;
No longer worthy is that one
    Who yields to look back from the plough.

Mother Dear, I'm not forgetting,
    In the turmoil of the throng,
How you bade me follow virtue,
    Choose the right: abhor the wrong.
E'er my thoughts you bade be guarding;
    Thought is parent of the deed:
Virtue is its own rewarding—
    Always turn to God in need.

Mother Dear, I'm not forgetting,
    In the sunset's glorious ray,
How you bade me think on home-ties,
    Stronger growing day by day;
And at night before I lay me
    Down to rest, to look above
Meekly bowing down before Him,
    Praying the Great God of Love.

Mother Dear, I'm not forgetting,—
    But the climb is long and drear,
Oft the mount-crag's fierce down-frowning
    Change most ardent hope to fear;

Yet the Crown for which I'm striving—
    Call my own? I could not dare!—
Mother Mine, to you I'll bring it;
    None but you that Crown shall wear!

The Gossip
or
The Old Maid's Story.

Come in!
Why, how d'ye do, dear Alice Nain!
Come to see me in all this rain?
Come in!—Draw close up to the fire.
How's all your folks and Aunt Maria?
Do let me make you some warm tea;
Your things are wet as they can be;—
You don't mind rain? So I've been told;
Some of these days you'll take a cold,
And then, for all this lack of gumption,
You'll have a nice case of consumption!
I'm so glad to see you! I declare
You're looking fine. Have this rocking chair;
Put your feet on the fender. What pretty shoes!
Do they turn dampness?
          But tell me the news—
I'm just dying to hear what the world is doing;
Who's been courting and who's been wooing.
Has Emma come? No? I thought not—
Too soon for her. The tea's almost hot.
Tell me of your Uncle Jake—
How much sugar do you take?
Will you have cream? Just help yourself.
I'll see what's out upon the shelf;—
Ah! here's some biscuit and some ham,
Some light bread, too—and this jam
Is very good. 'Twas the last I made;
It's 'most as rich as marmalade.
Tell me all about old Mrs. Birch;
Was she converted down at church?
How many converts has the Rev'rend Tabs made?

I certainly wish that church mortgage was paid.

Virginia is married! I knew that would thrill you!
Married a farmer—wouldn't that kill you!
They say when in school she was such a swell dresser;
Her cap, they all thought, was set for a professor.
Some girls had stayed single and died in regret;
It's not what you want always, but what you can get.

You remember that dress I bought last spring?
The goods was figured, something like a bird's wing.—
Well, last night I caught it on a tack,
And ripped the whole thing up the back!
You know that gown was some expense;
At a sale—twelve dollars and ninety-eight cents!
When I saw it all ruined so quick,
I sat down and cried;—it just made me sick.

I hear our village is to have a band;—
Twenty-four pieces! Won't that be grand!
I know Ash Hookins and that Munroe Heeder
Will give them a time; they'll both want to be leader.

Have you heard of the goings-on over at school?
Well, one of the teachers, Professor George Pool,
Has a girl in Birmingham,—so they say,—
And he writes to the blessed child every day.
I don't s'pose he ever will marry,—but then
You never can tell about some of these men.
Do you think he enjoys being bound in love's fetters?
I'd give half my life to see one of his letters.

Aunt Agnes' Baby is dead! 'Tis a shame!
It's better off, poor thing; 'twould have always been
    lame.
Didn't you know it had only one eye?
Well, it did, and something was wrong with its thigh!
Though I loved and pitied it, yet some repulsion
I experienced too. It died in a convulsion.

Miss Marie called yesterday. 'Tis a disgrace;
The powder that woman dabs onto her face.

One Sunday in church, I just thought I would scream,
She came in and the powder was thicker than cream;
And the airs she put on and the width of that dress
And laced up so tight, she looked like distress.
They say she is after old Bachelor Jim,
But if he sees her first, she'll never catch him.

    Have some of the jelly; it's not very thick;
Miss Thompson sent it when I was sick.
She's a good-hearted soul, tho' I don't understand her;
She never says much. That fat man Leander
Pays her attentions; he's quite a catch
And as queer as she is. Won't they make a match?

    But say, have you seen Miss Lou? Child, I declare,
I think 'twas last Wednesday; all her false hair
Somehow or other got caught in her hat,
And when the wind blew it off, I nearly fell flat.
The funny part was, that Jinny and Sam
Were coming along,—have some more ham,—
And Miss Lou heard them laugh and turned right
    about,
And gave those young folks a good setting out.
They looked so dumfounded; I thought I would die—
And Miss Lou was so angry!
        Do you know that I
Made two pies last week for my friend Mrs. Goff,
And the mice came and ate all the tops of them off.
I hate this old place for the live-long day;
Through the walls the rats and mice frolic and play;
And one night, just after I'd gotten in bed,
A great big old rat jumped right on my head!
I screamed so loud and made such a din,
That all the neighbors came rushing in;
And there I was in my night dress—
And the men came, too; "Did they stare?" Well, I
    guess!
Oh, laugh if you want to; just laugh 'till you shake;

But just imagine my feelings;
    Have some of the cake;
It's not very good, yet it's not very bad;
I think it fell somewhat; It seems kind o' sad.
I never have good luck with cakes at all;
I try but it seems they're determined to fall.
Speaking of falling,—you heard of course
About young Oscar Bennett; he fell from his horse.
I don't think he was hurt, save a scratch on his hand;
Fell in the garbage—nice place to land.
Pretty name for a horse, isn't it?—"Marguerite?"
They say in the races she wins every heat.
He's nice-looking; but sometimes good-lookers are
  fickle.
Do you fancy jockeys?
    Do try the pickle;
I canned them last fall by Miss Minnie's receipt;
It works like a charm.—Now aren't they sweet?
The cheese? I beg pardon, what was it you said?
Ah! don't say that, Dearie! Don't say "corn-bread!"
That word just sends a knife to my heart.
Whenever I hear it, I shudder and start
Like one pursued by a horrible dream.
See how excited! I've upset the cream!
There, there! It's wrong to give 'way, I know,
But that word turns loose such flood tides of woe,
That my soul cries out, though I'm sure that you
Meant no harm; but I thought everyone knew.
You don't? Well, list then, while with mem'ry's spade
I re-turn the past of a lonely old maid.

THE OLD MAID'S STORY.

Years ago I had a love, a noble youth was he,—
I loved him fondly, Alice, and I knew that he loved me.
We were betrothed—the cards were out—the wedding
    day was set—
And then that happened which has made my life one
    long regret;
There was not a bit of reason in it, that I'm bound to
    say;
But it happened as things happen, and it happened just
    this way:
He was going out of town to make a trade in property;
That very afternoon he called, half-jesting said to me:
"Why, Mary, I'm to be away; can't you fix me up a
    lunch?
"Make something with your own dear hands—just a
    bite to crunch
"While I'm on the train. You know I kind o' like
    cornbread;—
"Let's see what kind of cook you are"—the very words
    he said.
Well, I flew out in the kitchen; asked John to come
    out, too;
I was just so proud and happy to show him what I
    could do.
There was not one in the county, could cook so well
    as I;
And my forte was baking cornbread, after that came
    making pie.
'Twas in the oven in a minute and oh, I was so glad:
'Pride surely goeth 'fore a fall'—that cornbread turned
    out bad;
It was just so wet and soggy, though I'm sure that it
    was done;
John just roared with laughter—that's how it was begun;

For John he teased and taunted, and he guyed me and
 he joked;
In my shame and disappointment, Alice, well I got provoked.
At first I cried, then John he tried, of course, to make
things straight;
Wouldn't hear of going that night—insisted that he'd
 wait
And let me try again. Then he my pardon craved and
 plead;
But when he added: "I am sure you can at least make
 bread";—
That settled it. I screamed: "I hate you!" Yes, I did
 say "hate"—
"Get gone; the sooner the better—I don't want you to
 wait!"
My own words seemed to drive me on, for then I lost
 all grace,
And in a sudden passion threw the bread right in his
 face!
He never said a word, Alice, didn't even start,
But oh! the look he gave me, Child, cut me to the
 heart!
I'd rather he had struck me than to look at me that
 way.
He took his hat, picked up the bread,—in silence walked
away. I stood just where he left me; grief, anger, pride and
 shame,
All battling for possession—thus I stood till mother
 came.
And seeing my wild looks, something of the trouble
 guessed;
She took me in her arms; oh, how I sobbed upon her
 breast.
One consoling thought that coming somewhat eased the
 conscience rack;
"On the morrow I should see him—in the morn John

would come back."
How I vowed to beg forgiveness! Could I hope for his
    respect!
Ah, God! there was no morrow—the evening train was
    wrecked!
Can I e'er forget that hour—the hour when I was
    told?
My heart stopped short its beating, then I shook as if
    with cold.
We drove to where it happened; 'twas not many miles
    away;
And the scene that there I witnessed—no wonder I am
    gray.
All the train had twice turned over after it had left
    the track;
Then the wreckage caught on fire, though when we arrived
    'twas black;
But still 'twas slightly burning, giving out a lurid light
Which seemed to add new horrors to the darkness of
    the night.
'Twas a scene of awful carnage; half-burned bodies all
    around.
Scarce my lips could frame the question: "My John—
    has he been found?"
Was it hope that begged the answer; was it hope or
    Was it dread?
I prayed to find him living, but felt sure I'd find him
    dead.
When at last no traces of him caused hope to rise
    again—
'Twas short lived; section workers said they'd seen him
    on the train—
Then though kind hands had kept me, possessed by
    wild despair
Unmindful of all danger, I leapt down 'mid the wreckage
    there.

Oh! the horrors of that search, 'mid wild cries and
    mangled flesh!
Crawling where the twisted irons had formed a tangled
    mesh,
I found something—a man's hand! John's! I knew it
    by the ring;
That was all; but 'twas a moment 'fore I dared to touch
    the thing.
Not till I knelt and pressed it did I discover that the
    dead
Fingers of my lover were bespattered with cornbread!

I don't remember after that; I must have swooned or
    fainted.
When I came to, 'twas Spring again; folks' houses all
    were painted;
I could see them from my window as I lay there in my
    room;
And by the fragrance I could tell our lilacs were in
    bloom.
And while I lay and wondered, mother came in with
    some tea;
I looked and spoke; she said: "Thank God! my child's
    given back to me!"
That's all of it, Alice; now that you know,
You won't blame me perhaps for taking on so.
His was the only love I ever knew;
That's why I never have cornbread.
                But you
Are not going so soon? I thought you had stayed
A bit longer to cheer up a lonely old maid.
You have something for me? What is it? Let's see!
Why, you dear Sugar-lump! A package of tea!
I know I'll enjoy it. It is so kind
Of you to remember me. Well, never mind;
I'll repay you some day.

Yes, here's your jacket,—
Who's that at the gate, kicking up such a racket?
Oh, Dick's come for you, has he? That's suspicious,
    my Dear!
I'm glad it's stopped raining—the moon's shining clear.
The ground is still wet, but you'll need no umbrella.
Bid Maria come see me; my love to Aunt Ella,
And your mother and father. Kiss little Ben;
Be a good girl and come see me again!
    Good-night!

FINIS.

Citadel

Anna Minerva Henderson

PART ONE

A GARMENT OF PRAISE

*"I know not how the fields that gave us birth draw us with
sweetness, never to be forgotten, back through the dark."*
Alfred Noyes

MARKET SLIP

18 May, 1783

Voyaging, they came at last to land
Here in this sheltered inlet of the bay,
Curved like the hollow of a mighty hand,
The hills around, greening, and sweet with May.
This land was Spring, prescient of dreams fulfilled;
This land was life to the adventuring soul,
His to subdue and shape it as he willed,
The cherished dream of freedom as his goal.
O brave of heart, the eager, reaching tides
Besieged your shores, and inland singing trees
Reared barricades of beauty on all sides.
You took the challenge of the woods and seas
And captured in a single classic phrase
The moving story of those valiant days.

18 May, 1947

Time sifts out truth and this his verdict here—
Beauty for beauty ... Where the forests grew
In gay profusion, year on changing year,
A city stands, the gateway to a new
And untried world. And here will come one day
The Old World throngs, their hopes and dreams, to be
Tempered in the New World's alembic, they
No longer war-spent but at peace and free.
Dreamers and builders! This a dream's fruition ...
Fusing the present with the storied past,
To build a future of a broader vision,
To come to a new height and strength at last,
The beauty then of freedom and of power,
O Canada be great! This is your hour!

SAINT JOHN, NEW BRUNSWICK

"O fortunati, quorum
jam moenia surgunt."

Steep streets, tall spires etched against the sky,
Grey wharves that know the way of wind and tide,
Dim, drifting fog, the sea-gulls' plaintive cry,
A city, old, assured, wearing the pride
Of epic memories and heritage.
Like some brave odyssey the story reads,
Which they, who reared the walls and set the stage,
Imprinted here in gallant faith and deeds.
The heart remembers beauty in the spell
Of sailors' chanteys blown along the dark,
Of windy harbour lights and channel bell,
The sweep of sea and wings; nor fails to mark
The quiet strength that builds and reaches on ...
In the grey East, the cohorts of the Dawn!

THE OLD BURYING GROUND

Here the tall trees spread out protecting arms
And arch the sloping walks with leafy shade,
As though defending from the world's alarms
The quiet sleepers in their shelter laid.
Old men on benches talk the hours away
Through golden afternoons, and little know
The peace they find in watching children play,
The depths of healing beauty can bestow.
And though unheeded now, it surely seems
As if the hallowed dead still bear a part,
Leaving their legacy of faith and dreams
Forever graven on the city's heart—
A paradox of life and death, that pass
As light and shadow drift across the grass.

KING SQUARE

The heart of Saint John is King Square, laid out
Like the Union Jack, so in plan and name
(Though quite unconsciously there is no doubt)
Making to Loyalty a dual claim.
The Square's an active, interesting place,
And pleasant, as the seasons come and go,
Each making contribution of its grace,
From Spring's sweet promises to Winter's snow.
Monuments, fountain and a band-stand lend
Especial interest. On band-concert nights .
Everyone comes and stays until the end —
Or so it seems — a happy crowd! Street lights
Sparkle and fade, but twinkling stars look down
In benediction on a proud old town.

FOG

On tides of silence drifting like a cloud
The fog comes blotting out the sky and sea,
Veiling all clearness in a misty shroud
And lost to view are town and ships and quay.
All sound is muted and what seemed but now
A sudden distant rush of hurrying feet,
Was just the swaying of a foggy bough
Dashing staccato drops along the street.
It was like this before the world began,
This grayness, fluid yet opaque, and cold
With isolation … it could *be* that man
Came of God's loneliness. As years unfold,
Life's mysteries, like Earth by fog concealed,
Like Earth in lifting fog, may be revealed.

CORNER GROCERY STORE

As S.S. Pierce of Boston wisely said:
"A grocery store should have a corner site."
He knew whereof he spoke — a clever head.
This little store by accident was right.
Both twinkling windows held a brave array
Of sweets and penny goods — delightful things —
We gazed in wistfully at the display
With the frustrated hope that longing brings.
A bell clanged overhead soon as the door
Was opened ... A fat pug-dog blocked the way.
He sensed a timid child's brave nonchalance,
But the shop-keeper hushed the starting roar.
I haven't seen pug-dogs for many a day
And trust I won't in any circumstance.

In London — when we all were nearly grown —
The little shop a far-off memory —
I found its counterpart quite on my own.
The claim to individuality —
No dog (thank Heaven!) and a Dickens touch
That seemed almost to come alive for me.
The goods from everywhere! This could be such
A jolly place to learn geography!
Finding upon a busy thoroughfare
This shop in London-town of my delight,
Was like a story that I might have read,
And suddenly I thought as I stood there:
Oceans do not divide us, but unite.
It was like coming home when all was said.

A GARDEN REMEMBERED

Tall trees, aristocrats in form and pride
Grew there; drifts of gay flowers talked with me,
No maritime garden sea-fog drenched could hide
Its lovely fragrance breathing of the sea.
And so the garden lives within my heart
With the eternal things that do not fail,
Invisible, but there it has a part
And I can paint it to the last detail.
Today huge houses crowd the garden space,
Arrogant, stark, an economic boast.
Progress has turned a devastating face,
No loveliness is there. There is no ghost
Of the lost garden, of the beauty spent,
Save one tall tree bending as in lament.

PIONEER

Adventure claimed him.
The difficult, the danger-ridden,
He overcame as Jacob with the Angel,
And then his heart sang.
In vain his enemies
Strove to ensnare him
With the "*yoke of iron*
And the bands of brass".
Hurt, but undaunted, he pressed on.
Levels and foothills
In green and soft deception,
Tested his strength. The mountain
Took all of his strength and courage.
Often light guided him —
The Merlin Gleam. The air
Grew clearer, keener, as he climbed,
And when he reached the top,
An instant's light revealed
The world-road he had made.
He sank down welcoming release
In the kind dark
And the cool depths of peace.

PART TWO

PRAYER

*"I cannot praise a fugitive and cloistered virtue unexercised
and unbreathed, that never sallies out and sees her
adversary but slinks out of the race where that immortal
garland is to be run for not without dust and heat."*
—John Milton

Dear God, I ask not that along my way
The path be smoothed nor to direct my tread
The trail be blazed, a chart before me spread,
Nor that the dark too soon be turned to day.
The untried virtue shrinking in dismay
From life's turmoil, its bitterness, and dread,
I cannot praise. Where strength and Men are bred,
In dust and heat of conflict let me stay.
Teach me the truth that triumphs over pain.
Grant that to me the sweat of toil be sweet.
I ask no rich reward. I only crave
A spirit singing to the lashing rain,
A lifted heart that never knows defeat.
God help me to be strong! God make me brave!

MOUNT MANSFIELD, VERMONT

Up where the trail is lost against the sky
We climb exultant. The wide world is ours —
Beauty, majestic as a trumpet cry
Re-echoing from bastioned walls and towers;
And singing happiness. This now we know —
That nevermore can level valley-ways
Shrouded in mist and sheltered, far below,
Suffice to hold us captive through our days.
The winds that rioted all day are still
Hushed in the prescience of coming night,
A late moon rises over one tall hill
Drenching the world in floods of silver light,
And in the valley, dark in dreams below
Gleam here and there the twinkling lights of Stowe.

DEATH

When Death comes to my door in the end,
May there be naught of fear or surprise.
I would look on his face with calm eyes,
I would reach for his hand as a friend.

BOUQUET AND BRICKBAT

I could not sleep. Before I went to bed
I'd read "The Colyum"*. Need I further say
An old ambition that I thought was dead
Stalked forth — an adverse ghost I could not lay,
And urged me, not where gypsy trails are laid,
But where the hard road sometimes winds to fame
In close pursuit of Barrie's "darling jade"†
That in "The Colyum" I might find my name.
I could not sleep! The doctor, Coué-wise,
Chattered of force of will and then he said,
(Did I detect a twinkle in his eyes?)
"You ought to read before you go to bed,
Nothing exciting, something dull you know.
That Column with the caption, "J.A.O."

---

*   "The Colyum" "JUST AMONG OURSELVES" or "J.A.O." was
     the caption of a somewhat humorous column in the "Ottawa
     Citizen" some years ago.
†   J. M. Barrie described journalism as "that darling jade."

ST. MICHAEL AND ALL ANGELS

29th September
This is your day and so I bring
Roses you loved, and Michaelmas daisies
Gathered along the way.
The sky is gold in the West,
There is no bird song.
It is good that the weary day is ended.
It is good to rest.

PARLIAMENT HILL, OTTAWA

Like a departing conqueror, the sun
Goes in triumphant glory down the sky,
Taking the pointed towers one by one
With a brave loveliness in passing by.
The twilight shadows deepen on the snow,
The young moon swings, a slender golden arc
Above the town, and yellow street-lamps glow
Like crocuses against the purple dark.

And something of the life that throngs the street,
The essence of its laughter and its pain,
Of mounting dreams and triumphs and defeat,
Is woven in the carillon's refrain,
And lifted through the starlight clear and high
Is flung, transformed, a song against the sky!

THIS LIFE

This life, this gift unsought, so strangely mine,
Vouchsafes no answer question as I may
This fusion of the human and divine
That makes articulate the insensate clay.
Sometimes I've wondered if indeed 'twere best
Not to have lived, and craved an empty board
Devoid of viands, without Host or guest,
The lamp unlighted and the wine unpoured.
But the mood passed. I who have walked alone
With hate and fear, and quelled them in my hour
With level steadfast gaze, now claim my own:
Mine is the glory, ay, and mine the power!
Serenity and strength to me belong,
Their alchemy transmuting pain to song.

CHRISTMAS-PARTY FOR ENGLAND[*]
OYEZ! OYEZ! OYEZ!

Here's the Message of the Crier of the Town,
Read the Words across, the First Letters down.

"Christmas in England," still that simple phrase
Holds all the magic of the long ago —
Revel and Yule log, singing Waits and snow,
In Merrie England of old peaceful days.
So though war's shadow darkens the loved land
That gave us Dickens and his Christmas Tales
Mingled with cheer, his spirit still prevails
A light among us, guiding heart and hand,
Shining through us may yet make England bright.

Perchance the beam will glow throughout the years,
And we can all through laughter and our tears
Repeat with joyful hearts on Christmas night
The Dickens grace that crowns the deed well done,
Yuletide and Peace — "God bless us, everyone."

[*] Written for a "Bundles for Britain" Christmas party held at the
National Museum, Ottawa, some years ago.

THE LACEMAKER

Springtime without. A little laughing tree
New-leaved and April-fragrant after rain,
Tossed dancing shadows through the window-pane
Across her work — a cobweb tracery
Of fairy stitches … Came a sudden thrill
Of piercing sweetness in a robin's note,
She paused. Her slim hands fluttered to her throat
She bowed her head upon the window-sill,
And singing memories awoke and died —
The shining dreams of youth that Life denied.

PEACE

I come at the end
And soothe the final agonies of strife
With a white radiance. My light
Turns the soul of darkness
To the glory of dawn,
Bringing new strength, and courage.
I am an end and a beginning.
I am Peace.

DEPARTURE

Parenthesis

She had smiled, when he left,
In a casual way
And he never knew
What her heart longed to say.

But when the door closed
She rushed to the hall
Then stood there so still
One could hear a pin fall.   *Similar to God's in ... ...*

For she sensed the long years
And her heart's bitter lack   → *Lack thereof is bitter*
                               → *Contradiction of a lack, void,*
But she knew it was best   *bitter*
That he should not come back.
                               'Lack why in a ... any
                               to NAUGHT

She'll remember forever
The great hall clock,
The ironical cadence,   → *Stuck in time*
The eternal tick-tock.   → *stuck in silence*
                          → *Forever → no change*
                          → *stagnant but also*
                          change

PRAYER-MEETING

Revivals and long winter nights
Seemed to go hand in hand.
The villagers found strength in the first
The latter to withstand.

The brightly lighted meeting-house
With all the neighbours there,
The comradeship and singing
Eased the daily load of care.

That night — the service had begun —
A frightful storm arose,
The snow was stinging powdered ice
That swirled in drifts and froze.

The meeting-house was bright and warm,
The Deacon knelt to pray,
When from her seat and down the aisle,
Marched Sister Susie Gray,

Out in the storm and banged the door
With a resounding thud.
The Deacon waxed more eloquent,
His words poured in a flood.

Over the old south meadow lot
They'd quarreled, and Susie said
She'd never listen to his voice
Though she "should be struck dead."

And so the Deacon prayed and prayed,
The folk were ill at ease,
Never was heard so long a prayer,
'Twas hard upon the knees,

But harder still on Susie Gray
We shivered for her there
And wondered if she could survive
That masterpiece in prayer.

At long last even prayers must end.
With a wild gust of snow
Stiffly but gamely, Susie came
In to the warmth and glow.

The tangy salt sea breeze down East
Preserves a hardy folk,
That night of seeming tragedy
Became a standing joke.

CROW AND CRITIC

Winter had gone like an absconding tenant,
Quietly, stealthily, save for the passionate
Almost indignant outbursts of wind and rain
Sweeping away all traces.
Spring moved in over night, and today
Patches of soft green appeared
Between the red bricks of the street.
The sky was cloudlessly blue, and the air
Laden with fragrance of growing things,
Seemed all colour and light.
Over the way a crow wheeled and circled.
Contrary to the usual opinion of crows
This one could be called beautiful.
Its feathers glistened and scintillated in the sun,
And flapping majestically it came to rest
On the steeple ball of the old Lutheran Church.
Service was being held and the singing
In great waves of glorious sound
Came to me in my window,
The crow, looking down with its head on one side
Listened intently and — could it have been? —
With intelligence and enjoyment.

It was a Spring day at its best and I made a poem
Of what I saw from my window,
Including, of course, the crow.
The Critic said: "The Crow flapping seems to be
A digression. What does it really contribute
To the meaning of the poem?"
I might have quoted Archibald MacLeish
"A poem should not mean, but be."
But replied: "It was part of the picture
I saw from my window, so I put it in."

I had not then heard of Dylan Thomas's poem
And *his* crow. I was glad it was part
Of the picture he saw from *his* window,
And that he, too, "Put it in."
I am not, however, buying a blind
For my window.

THE REFLECTIONS OF AN ECCLESIASTICAL BIRD-WATCHER (Winter 1965)

George Washington "worshipped" here but he did not
    "sleep" ...
(Sermons then being almost as good as today).
The Church is Colonial and a treasure, to keep,
And "watching" to this end's the only available way.
Though our knowledge was slight, my predecessor and I
Talked of the "new theology" and of prayer,
Indifferent if God dwells "down", "out", or "on high",
Provided He is, as of old, everywhere.
Blake's picture of God as a bearded old man
And H.G. Wells' concept ... 'a beautiful youth" ...
Are wholly inadequate. No mortal can
Portray God who transcends even "beauty and truth",

Then I was alone. If the turn of a phrase
Can capture the comfort and utter release
Of this place from the clamor of our troubled days,
It might read: A haven of infinite peace.

Visitors? Yes.
The first was a lady who quietly prayed;
Another performed altar duties a while;
Came a man whose remarks praising "watchers" were made;
Then the Rector passed through
With a friendly word and a smile.
There came a long pause. Then, ah then! the door
Stealthily opened, though not on its own.
A swift rush of cold air swept from pew-top to floor
But nobody entered. I still was alone.
Mysteries are intriguing and I *would* not look.
I enjoyed it. The door closed again without sound
And stealthily still — a mystery book

Could not have done better. Shall I ever be found
In a like situation — playing the host
To so unceremonious and wintry a ghost?
Perhaps someone in far-away 2065
May find the recorded list — it would be long —
Of "watchers" and bring the story alive.
Then we, too, historically, would belong.

Notes

The Album of a Heart by Robert Nathaniel Dett was originally published by Mocowat-Mercer / Lane College in 1911. Copyright ©1911 by Robert Nathaniel Dett.

Citadel authored by Anna Minerva Henderson copyright © 1967. Used with permission under a non-exclusive license issued by the Copyright Board of Canada.

Clarence and Corinne; or, God's Way by Amelia Etta Hall Johnson was originally published by the American Baptist Publication Society in 1890. Copyright ©1890 by Amelia Etta Hall Johnson.

About the Editor

PHOTO: Department of English, Harvard University.

The 4th Poet Laureate of Toronto (2012-15) and 7th Parliamentary Poet Laureate (2016-17), George Elliott Clarke is a revered artist in song, drama, fiction, screenplay, essays, and poetry. Now teaching African-Canadian literature at the University of Toronto, Clarke has taught at Duke, McGill, the University of British Columbia, and Harvard. He holds eight honorary doctorates, plus appointments to the Order of Nova Scotia and the Order of Canada. His recognitions include the Pierre Elliott Trudeau Fellows Prize, the Governor-General's Award for Poetry, the National Magazine Gold Award for Poetry, the Premiul Poesis (Romania), the Dartmouth Book Award for Fiction, the Eric Hoffer Book Award for Poetry (US), and the Dr. Martin Luther King Jr. Achievement Award. Clarke's work is the subject of *Africadian Atlantic: Essays on George Elliott Clarke* (2012), edited by Joseph Pivato.